QUALITY MANAGEMENT
for Projects and Programs

Lewis R. Ireland
Fellow, PMI

A Publication of the Project Management Institute
14 Campus Boulevard
Newtown Square, Pennsylvania 19073 USA
610/356-4600 Fax: 610/356-4647
E-mail: customercare@pmi.org
Internet: www.PMI.org

Library of Congress Cataloging-in-Publication Data

Ireland, Lewis R., 1937–
        Quality management in projects and programs/Lewis R. Ireland.
                p.   cm   .—(Perspectives in project and program management series)
                "A publication of the Project Management Institute
                Includes bibliographical references.
        ISBN 1-880410-11-7
                1. Total quality management.   2. Industrial project management.
I. Project Management Institute.   II. Title.   III. Series.
        658.5'62–dc20   91-26905
                                                                                                CIP

ISBN 978-1-880410-11-0

Published by: Project Management Institute, Inc.
                            14 Campus Boulevard
                            Newtown Square, Pennsylvania 19073-3299 USA
                            Phone: +1-610-356-4600
                            Fax: +1-610-356-4647
                            E-mail: customercare@pmi.org
                            Internet: www.PMI.org

PMI Publications welcomes corrections and comments on its books. Please feel free to send comments on typographical, formatting, or other errors. Simply make a copy of the relevant page of the book, mark the error, and send it to: Book Editor, PMI Publications, Four Campus Boulevard, Newtown Square, PA 19073-3299 USA.

To inquire about discounts for resale or educational purposes, please contact the PMI Book Service Center:

                            PMI Book Service Center
                            P.O. Box 932683, Atlanta, GA 31193-2683 USA
                            Phone: 1-866-276-4764 (within the U.S. or Canada)
                            or 1-770-280-4129 (globally)
                            Fax: 1-770-280-4113
                            E-mail: book.orders@pmi.org

Foreword

In the products we buy, in the work we perform, and in the manner in which we live our lives, each of us has an image or an interpretation of what the word "quality" means. These images and interpretations are shaped by national, cultural, religious, corporate, and family values and the expectations that flow from these values. Varied as our expectations may be, a productive process, or way of doing something has "quality" when it meets or satisfies those expectations, so it's not surprising that the definition of quality appears to be both simple and elusive.

In this publication, *Quality Management for Projects and Programs*, Lew Ireland has tackled this challenge with the perspective of years of practical, professional experience as well as the wisdom gained from his academic pursuits. As such he focuses on the concept "do the right thing right the first time" and what it takes to achieve this in projects and programs. Understanding the customer's requirements and the essential nature of planning to meet these expectations is explored thoroughly, and there is solid discussion of the quality variables—the choice of resources, the human factors, the effects of internal and external demands, the tools, the management techniques, the methodologies, and the costs—associated with infusing quality into projects management.

Since enhanced productivity, less rework, lower costs, and better customer acceptance all flow from early planning for quality management, strong competition has forced many companies to re-examine, among other things, the emphasis, internal education, and support given to quality management as an everyday part of all business functions. It has also forced them to re-evaluate the costs associated not only with infusing quality programs and attitudes into everyday business conduct but also the costs associated with not doing so.

Lew Ireland and contributing authors, Dr. Francis M. Webster, Jr. and Sandra Kay Fenton, have constructed a solid presentation for investing quality in project management from the planning through the control and reporting methodologies.

"Robust" has been a term used to describe an essential quality characteristic, but I prefer "vitality" because it conveys both the sense of a product's ability to meet performance specifications **and** its durability. While new contributions to knowledge are a fortunate part of life, I believe this fine publication makes a vital contribution to quality management from which both experienced personnel and newcomers to project management can benefit.

Mary Devon O'Brien
President, Project Management Institute

Preface

Quality Management for Projects and Programs is addressed in seven chapters and four appendices. The chapters provide the background for quality, the planning requirements, the costs associated with quality (and non-quality), the customer's requirements, statistical concepts and other tools, and the people involvement in quality. Although the information contains many examples of quality in a manufacturing environment, this is for illustrative purposes only to reflect ongoing efforts in quality management. The concepts are pertinent to the project environment with some minor tailoring to the type of work being accomplished under varying conditions.

The appendices contain stand-alone information, i.e., the check list for the Malcolm Baldrige National Quality Award, the check list for the Deming Prize (Overseas), a glossary of terms, and a bibliography of pertinent literature. This information is essential to the understanding of quality in projects and the trend of improving productivity through continuous quality improvement.

All aspects of quality are not covered in this book because of the many diverse and unique approaches to implementing quality programs between countries, industries, and organizations. For example, the Japanese methods are different from those practiced in Germany or the United States. Therefore, the initiation of any quality management program may need to be supplemented from additional literature and authoritative sources to tailor the program to meet individual and company requirements. The bibliography lists sources of information that may be suitable for supplementing the available knowledge.

Acknowledgments

The author gratefully acknowledges the efforts of others who have contributed to the successful completion of this book. The author accepts all responsibility for the accuracy and completeness of the material.

Contributing Authors

Dr. Francis M. Webster, Jr., Western Carolina University, Cullowhee, North Carolina, for his contribution to the concept of a project in Chapter 3 and for his overall contribution to the general outline of the book. He presented the first PMI Quality Management in Projects workshop at the 1985 Seminar/Symposium in Denver. The concepts developed and presented in that and subsequent workshops provided the basic framework from which the outline for this book was derived.

Ms. Sandra Kay Fenton, MCI, Alexandria, Virginia, for her contribution to the statistical concepts in Chapter 5, and for her critique of other chapters.

Typing and Editorial Support

Ms. Ouida F. Ireland, Reston, Virginia, for preparing the final manuscript and editing the many draft copies.

Reviewers

Mr. William Duncan, PMP – Duncan Associates, Lexington, MA
Mr. Ed Grizer, PMP   – Kodak Corporation, Rochester, NY
Dr. Tim Kloppenborg   – Xavier University, Cincinnati, OH
Dr. Chris Stylianides   – North Dakota State University, Fargo, ND
Mr. Robert Templeton   – The M.W. Kellogg Company, Houston, TX

Dedication

Dee – Whose perseverance sets an example.

Dean – Never a Spectator, always a Gladiator. Project Management is not a spectator's sport.

Contents

Chapter I   The Quality Movement

Chapter II   Dimensions of Customer Requirements

Chapter III   Planning for Quality in Projects

Chapter IV   Cost of Quality

Chapter V   Statistical Concepts and Quality Tools

Chapter VI   Quality and People in Project Management

Chapter VII   Achieving Project Quality

Appendices

Illustrations

Quality management is receiving increased attention because it is one of the major contributors to changes in productivity. Companies are seeking new methods to change the productivity equation in their favor. This chapter highlights some of the ongoing efforts and the need to embrace a quality program in companies and projects. Examples of industry efforts in the quality arena are used to show forward motion to meet the quality challenges, including achieving quality at plus/minus six sigmas, i.e., only a few parts per million defects.

Chapter I   The Quality Movement

A. The Quality Trend

The trend toward providing "quality products or services" has changed over the past forty five years from a gradual improvement orientation to one of demands by customers for quality. Because of today's international economic competition where products and services cross international borders with less difficulty, this trend is more visible than any time in the past. Countries are "specializing" in products and services that they can market to other countries while completely avoiding the development of other products and services. The reason that certain products and services are avoided is that they can be purchased at a cost less than they can be produced.

Japan, Korea, Taiwan, Hong Kong, and other Pacific Rim countries are providing goods to North American countries that meet customers' requirements and provide a satisfaction not obtained from domestic goods. Many Pacific Rim country exports have been in electronic equipments at the low-unit-cost end of the product market. Japan and Korea have also challenged the North American automobile market with small cars that are economical to purchase and operate. Europe, Great Britain, France, and Germany have challenged the North American automobile market with prestige cars that compete with the Cadillac, Lincoln, and Chrysler. Their success has not been as noticeable as the smaller automobiles produced by Japan and Korea, but there is a significant portion of the prestige automobile market going to European manufacturers.

The People's Republic of China stands as a major competitor to the Pacific Rim countries because of large stockpiles of natural resources and an abundance of human resources. The Chinese do not currently possess the sophistication to produce high-technology products that compete with Japan, Korea, Taiwan, and Hong Kong, but are moving in that direction. China currently exports human resources to work on projects in Argentina and Saudi Arabia.

These examples of countries exporting products and services that are major competitive efforts with the United States, and to some extent Canada, are based on their ability to provide customer satisfaction through a quality orientation. The products and services meet the needs of the customers and are considered quality goods by these consumers. The goal for the other countries is to provide competitive products and services that exceed the Pacific Rim and European countries' currently delivered goods at an equivalent price.

B. Global Competition

Continual importation of products into countries on the North American continent reflects a major imbalance in the international balance of payments. Importing countries suffer from a serious monetary situation where imports outweigh exports and a deficit situation is generated. This economic decline by importing nations has a lower limit whereby the country must take action to change this trend.

There are outcries to impose embargoes or tariffs that will place the exporting country at a disadvantage when competing with domestic products.

This solution seems simple on the surface, but has serious pitfalls when viewed as part of the global economy. Increased tariffs or embargoes restrict trade on exports as well as imports, which provides a net change in the balance of trade that may be less favorable than the current situation.

Improvement of position in the global market is best achieved through becoming more competitive in the price of products relative to their value. Changing this competitive position can be achieved through increased productivity in the fabrication of products. That is, the equation where input equals output must be shifted to where the same input equals increased output. A quality program can provide this shift in productivity.

In analyzing the competitive nature of products and services, it is fundamental to the comparison that the customer's requirements must be of prime importance. The customer's expectations and how they are managed determine whether the customer is satisfied. Quality in a product or service is, therefore, the degree to which the customer's requirements and expectations are satisfied.

Utility. This is a consumer expectation and requirement. Utility is the capacity of a product to be used for its intended purpose. The ease and the degree of completeness with which the product accomplishes the intended function is its relative utility. There is no real measure of utility that is generally accepted for all products. Therefore, utility must be measured in terms of relative degrees of satisfying the required purpose of the product.

Financial. The financial analysis must encompass all cost areas for a product or service. These cost areas include the cost to design and build, the cost to deliver, often the cost to operate and maintain, and the cost for warranty. Other costs can range from loss of sales through poor product or service image, litigation from sale of unsafe products, and public relations costs to mend damages caused by poor products or services. These costs should be used in analyses to determine, first, the price of the product, and second, the exposure to cost risk through delivery of a product or service that fails to meet minimum acceptable standards. Providing a product or service that meets the customer's requirements will diminish many of the secondary cost areas to insignificant levels and minimize cost risk exposure.

Legal. Legal issues range from regulatory agency violations to unlawful marketing of products that can cause injury. The litigation that may result from apparent or actual safety hazards in products can materially affect the competitive nature of products and can cause serious loss of revenue.

C. National Quality Incentives

Many countries recognize the need for quality although programs may not be fully implemented within the country's businesses to build products and services that can compete in an international arena. The incentive to build products and services that will sell in the international marketplace can be achieved through formal recognition programs established by governments and professional societies. Most notable are two awards that have achieved prominent recognition and acclaim: The Deming Prize (Overseas) and the Malcolm Baldrige National Quality Award.

Deming Prize (Overseas)

This award, administered by the Union of Japanese Scientists and Engineers (JUSE), is awarded to overseas companies that demonstrate a superior quality program. The criteria for the Deming Prize (Overseas) are contained in Appendix A.

The Deming Prize (Overseas) was awarded to Florida Power and Light Company of Juno Beach, Florida, in November 1989, the first to a non-Japanese company. This award was in recognition of Florida Power and Light Company's

Quality Improvement Program which has installed a management system that focuses on customer satisfaction.

Malcolm Baldrige National Quality Award

On August 20, 1987, the U.S. enacted Public Law 100-107, The Malcolm Baldrige National Quality Improvement Act, to establish an annual U.S. National Quality Award [165]. The purpose of this Act is to promote quality awareness, to recognize quality achievements of U.S. companies, and to publicize successful quality strategies. The criteria for the Malcolm Baldrige National Quality Award are shown in Appendix B.

The first awards were made in 1988 to Motorola, Incorporated; Commercial Nuclear Fuel Division, Westinghouse Corporation; and Globe Metallurgical, Incorporated. The summary of the award to Motorola is in paragraph I.F, page I - 8.

In 1989, there were two awards. Milliken & Company, headquartered in Spartanburg, South Carolina, produces more than 48,000 different textile and chemical products ranging from apparel fabrics and automotive fabrics to specialty chemicals and floor coverings. Milliken's quality program, "Pursuit of Excellence," has resulted in a 42 percent increase in productivity between 1980 and 1988

Xerox Business Products and Systems was the recipient of the other 1989 award. Headquartered in Stamford, Connecticut, Xerox attributes its success in turning around a declining world market for its products to the quality program "Leadership through Quality." Determining customer wants in its more than 250 document processing equipments, Xerox uses detailed analysis of its 375 information management systems to plan new products and services.

In 1990, there were four winners of the Malcolm Baldrige National Quality Award: (1) Cadillac Motor Car Company, (2) IBM Rochester, (3) Federal Express Corporation, and (4) Wallace Company, Inc. These winners represent automobile manufacturing (Cadillac Motor Car Company), computer hardware and software manufacturing (IBM Rochester), a service company (Federal Express Corporation), and a material distributor (Wallace Company, Inc.). Each achieved the honor through individually developed and implemented quality programs to meet the customers' requirements for products and services.

Cadillac Motor Car Company recognized a decline in its market share in the early 1980s. Initiating a program of simultaneous engineering teams to meet or exceed potential buyer expectations, Cadillac integrated customers, employees, suppliers, and dealers to focus on quality improvements. External suppliers were assigned "targets for excellence" in quality, cost, delivery, technology, and management for continuous improvement. Through these efforts, Cadillac is attracting new car buyers while having the highest repeat buyers in the automobile industry.

IBM Rochester, employing more than 8,100 people, links its success to analysis of current and potential customer needs and expectations. Customers are included in every aspect from design to delivery. Managers and operators are assigned quality improvement goals as a matter of routine business. IBM strengthened its quality initiatives by formulating six critical success factors: (1) improved product and service requirement definition, (2) enhanced product strategy, (3) six-sigma defect limit (or 3.4 defects per million), (4) further cycle time reductions, (5) improved education, and (6) increased employee involvement and ownership.

Federal Express employs approximately 90,000 people at more than 1,650 sites to process 1.5 million daily shipments. This translates to more than three million customers (shipper and receiver) per day, some with multiple packages. Federal Express's customer satisfaction is high and the company has initiated a program of twelve Service Quality Indicators, tied to customer expectations, to measure and improve the service. The goal of Federal Express employees is a 100 percent service standard in meeting customers' expectations.

Wallace Company, Inc., is relatively small in size with ten offices and 280 associates. All 280 associates are trained in quality improvement concepts and methods to implement Wallace's 1985 program for continuous quality improvement. The goal of "total customer satisfaction" resulted in Wallace setting new standards for service, establishing "partnerships" with customers and suppliers, and merging business and quality goals. Between 1987 and 1989, Wallace's sales volume increased by 67 percent, and operating profits increased by 7.4 percent.

D. Definitions of Quality Terms

Quality management, to be fully understood, must be defined and related terms must also be defined. The most commonly used terms and definitions are contained in Appendix C.

Quality has been defined from many different perspectives and has taken on meanings based on the private industry or government agency using the term. In its purest form:

"Quality is the totality of features and characteristics of a product or service that bear on its ability to satisfy stated or implied needs." [179, 2]

The term "quality" is not used to express a degree of excellence in a comparative sense nor is it used in a quantitative sense for technical evaluations. The more precise term is "relative quality" for the comparison or ranking of products. In the quantitative sense, "quality level" or "quality measure" is used during technical evaluations.

In some industries, government agencies, and educational institutions, quality is described as "fitness for use," "fitness for purpose," "customer satisfaction," or "conformance to the requirements." These terms are the goals of quality programs, not the definition of quality.

Fitness for use. Used to describe the product or service when it is provided to the customer. If a product or service is capable of being used, it is assumed that it will provide the customer the economic satisfaction desired.

Fitness for purpose. Similar to fitness for use in that the product or service will meet its intended purpose in all respects and provide the customer economic satisfaction.

Customer satisfaction. Describes the customer's feelings about a product or service. When the product or service meets the customer's expectations and provides the belief that the product or service has economic value.

Conformance to the requirements. Used to describe the condition of the product or service in relation to the customer's requirements. If the product conforms to the customer's requirements, it is assumed to be precisely what the customer desires.

The modern concepts of quality focus heavily on customer satisfaction and conformance to the (customer's) requirements more than fitness for use or purpose. This is not to say any of the concepts should be totally discarded, but that the terms may be used to convey different meanings during the total cycle of product and service development, fabrication, testing, operation and maintenance, and disposal stages.

Conformance to the customer's requirements is the best term to be used in a concept of building or operating a product because it focuses attention on elements of work to be accomplished to meet requirements or specifications.

The term "customer satisfaction" best describes the goal of a project or company in its relationship with the customer, from initial contact through delivery of the product or service. In modern quality concepts, fitness for use or purpose does not describe the intention of bringing customer satisfaction or of conforming to the customer's requirements and, therefore, has little relationship to current quality trends.

E. Quality Concepts

Zero Defects

"Zero defects" states that there is no tolerance for errors within the system. The goal of all processes is to avoid defects in the product or service.

In the initial development of quality concepts, it was assumed that any system or process would produce errors or defects because that was a fact of life. Management, therefore, set an allowable number of defects for any process or procedure. This was usually in the range of two or three percent, but could often be significantly more. Zero defect programs were instituted as slogans to be placed on bulletin boards and letterheads. Little was done to attempt to achieve a defect-free environment. An example is the slogan on the bottom of a letter received from the government "The Year of Zero Defects" and the letter was dated March 36, 1976 (sic).

More recently, zero defect programs have been re-established as goals for a defect-free environment. This is currently translated to mean "the goal is to provide products or services free of all defects" and there is no allowance for error in any process or procedure. Motorola, Inc., is attempting to achieve nearly defect-free products and services with a six-sigma goal, or errors of less than 3.4 defects per million units, as described in subsequent paragraphs in this chapter.

The Customer is the Next Person in the Process

This concept is based on providing the internal organization a system that ensures the product or service is transferred to the next person in the process in a complete and correct manner. The product or service being built is transferred to another internal party only after it meets all the specifications and all actions at a work station are complete. The next person in the process is entitled to receive a partial product or service upon which he can perform his operation or procedure.

This avoids incorrectly assembled components and poor workmanship. It is a subset of "conformance to the requirements" and "customer satisfaction" when the next person in the process is considered the customer. This approach avoids a situation such as in the assembly of missiles where the wires were installed and twisted, but not soldered before the cover was installed by another person. The poor wire connections were not discovered under static testing, but failure occurred most of the time during actual firings (a form of dynamic testing with gravitational forces acting on the missile) [162, 24].

Do the Right Thing Right the First Time (DTRTRTFT)

DTRTRTFT states that it is easier and less costly to do the work right the first time than it is to do it a second time. This concept entails the training of personnel to ensure they know how to correctly do the work and that they have the skills and tools to correctly complete the work. Moreover, people must be motivated to properly perform the work.

During a visit to Hughes Aircraft Company in California, a manager explained the concept being used in a job shop environment. There were nearly 100 percent rejects on sophisticated sighting devices being built for the U.S. Army. The rework effort was extremely expensive because of the disassembly of the devices for inspection and testing as well as replacement of defective

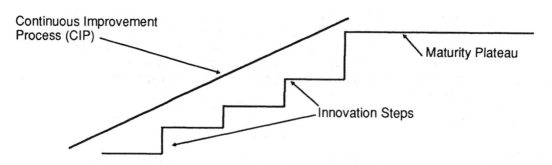

Figure I.1. Continuous Improvement Process and Innovation

parts. The decision was made to establish a process whereby all the parts were tested for defects after each integration to ensure the device was in working order at the completion of each operation. This gave the operators time to assemble the parts correctly and the testing gave the confidence that they were doing it right the first time.

Continuous Improvement Process

The continuous improvement process (CIP) is a concept which recognizes that the world is constantly changing and any process that is satisfactory today may well be unsatisfactory tomorrow[87]. The rapid changes to technology over the past forty years and the potential for more dramatic changes in the next ten years show the need to manage the change of processes to meet competition and excel in a dynamic environment. Projects as well as manufacturing need to recognize the situation as an opportunity to be the most competitive in a world marketplace.

The CIP is sustained, gradual change to improve the situation and, unlike innovation, does not make a sudden jump to a plateau where it matures over time. Innovation's giant leaps forward are like stair steps with the step surface being the maturation period. The CIP is the constancy of purpose whereby the technology is transformed to achieve maturity along with continual improvement.

CIP is a holistic approach to an organization that focuses on eleven principles while making the process improvements. These principles are: (1) constancy of purpose, (2) commitment to quality, (3) customer focus and involvement, (4) process orientation, (5) continuous improvement, (6) system-centered management, (7) investment in knowledge, (8) teamwork, (9) conservation of human resources, (10) total involvement, and (11) perpetual commitment. These principles are viewed as being compatible and mutually supportive for any organization to implement the CIP.

The most important change for project personnel and decision makers who influence the project is thinking of a project as a process. Rather than manage the output of a project, management is focused on the total process and subprocesses. In this manner, the process is held constant after it has been proven capable of the work and the product will naturally meet the requirements.

A simple example of managing a process is baking a cake. The recipe is followed by measuring and mixing all ingredients to the proper consistency. There are no substitutions or incorrect measurements. The proper mixing subprocess is used for the specified duration to meet a stated consistency. A cake pan is coated with cooking oil and filled with the mixture. The oven, heated to the proper temperature, receives the cake mixture for baking for a stated period of time. The next step is to remove the cake from the oven and allow it to cool before extracting it from the pan. To finish the process, there is a subprocess called icing the cake. Icing is prepared and uniformly distributed over the cake.

If the recipe (process) is followed, the oven is heated to the correct temperature during the warm-up period and for the cooking subprocess, and the icing procedures (subprocess) are followed, it is reasonable to assume the cake will conform to the texture, taste, size, and aroma specified in the recipe. This procedure replicated several times while the process is held constant should give similar end products (cakes). If the process varies, say for example the temperature decreases, the cake will not conform to the specification (recipe).

In a continuous improvement process, our example serves to show that we may want to change the texture and flavor to meet a customer's changing taste. Therefore, we modify the process (recipe) by changing the input subprocess (i.e., replacement or new ingredients). The baking process (temperature and bake duration) may also be adjusted to change the texture. This change to transform an existing process into a new process is the method of creating a new product. We do not, in this situation, think in terms of changing the inputs (ingredients, duration for baking, temperature), but focus on baking a cake as a process that controls the resultant end product.

The CIP is a concept that is applicable to projects because it supports the quality goals by making gradual improvements in the processes and subprocesses. When the project is viewed and managed as a process, the numerous subprocesses tend to repeat themselves over several projects, or often within a project. The procedure for this is as follows:

Define and standardize (sub)processes. Document current understanding; maintain and update formal standards; measure performance against current standards.

Assess (sub)process performance. Measure process; assess performance against goals and customer needs; select improvement targets.

Improve (sub)processes. Use teams for shared processes; pursue individual improvement; follow improvement cycle of standardize–do–check–act. The standardize–do–check–act procedure is similar to the Deming Wheel of Plan–Do–Check–Act.

Measure progress. Measure performance against goals and standards; evaluate customer satisfaction; evaluate method and document results; continuously improve.

The post-project evaluation is an excellent opportunity to identify the processes that need improvement and standardize them for future use and evaluation. The standard can serve as a guide to the project manager and team members during the planning and execution of the project as well as reduce nonconformance resulting from deviation from proven work practices.

Process Capability

In evaluating the processes which will be used to produce a system (product or service), it is essential that the process be capable of performing the required functions to achieve the desire outcome. Processes must have the capability to produce the specified item, component, material, or assembly. Following are examples of process capabilities.

Precision. A milling machine must be capable of more precise grinding than the required specification. If a part is to be milled to within plus or minus one one-thousandth of an inch, the milling machine must have a precision greater than one one-thousandth of an inch.

Capacity. A mixing machine must mix 9,600 pounds of ingredients in an eight-hour shift. The mixing machine must be rated at a capacity or at least 1,200 pounds for each hour of operation to have the minimum capacity to meet the process requirements. If there are interruptions in the mixing process, there may be a requirement for a much larger machine to produce more than 1,200 pounds each hour of operation.

Temperature. A bonding process requires the ambient temperature to be between 58 and 78 degrees Fahrenheit or the bonding will not be complete. The control of the temperature for the duration of the bonding process is a part of the process and can contribute to improper bonding of the parts. The control of the temperature must consider cooling if the temperature rises to 78 degrees or heating if the temperature decreases to 58 degrees. The heating and cooling capacity of devices maintaining the ambient temperature must be considered during the planning of the process.

Chemical compositions. Developing photographic film requires the proper mix of chemicals to "etch" the image into the film base. A weak solution will not complete all the image outlines while a strong solution will "burn" away the image outlines, commonly called under- and over-developing, respectively. Maintaining the solution within the acceptable range of chemical composition is required to ensure the desired photographic results.

All process capability planning requires a standard, a means to measure the standard, and a means to correct any variations. The standard is usually specified by an authoritative body, such as an industry standard. Measurement of the process must have the precision to assure the performance is within the specified parameters. The means to correct variances is any action from repair to adjustable controls for the process.

F. Quality Program Examples

Several industries and governmental agencies have initiated internal quality programs that are tailored to meet each activity's needs. The representative examples of the quality efforts show overall trends toward increasing quality across the industry or agency. The following industry examples are representative of recent quality movement milestones.

Electronic

Motorola, Incorporated, an electronics equipment manufacturer with over 100,000 employees worldwide, was the recipient of the 1988 Malcolm Baldrige National Quality Award [124]. Motorola's entire corporate system was placed under scrutiny before this award was earned.

In 1981, Motorola established a goal to improve the quality by ten times before 1986. The first major roadblock to achieving a tenfold improvement was the diversity of quality metrics, or system of quality measures, between Motorola's operating divisions. Three and one-half years into the five-year goal, Motorola established a single quality metric for all divisions, i.e., Total Defects per Unit.

A unit was defined as any unit of work to be applied to product or service and a defect was defined as anything which caused customer dissatisfaction, whether specified or not. An item of equipment, a circuit board assembly, a page of technical manual, a line of software code, an hour of labor, a wire transfer of funds, and any output an organization produced are examples of a unit .

Managers were skeptical of this ambitious goal for quality improvement, but in the process of improvement had to find new ways to perform the manufacturing operations. They also worked toward Motorola's practice of "Management by Measurement." Management by measurement required the establishment of measurements which correlate with the desired end result and regularly reviewed the actual measurements. The organization focused on those actions necessary to achieve the required improvement.

By 1986, using the uniform quality metric, Total Defects per Unit, one sector of Motorola exceeded the ten times improvement goal. The uniform quality metric was adopted as a company-wide measurement to permit uniform comparison of results and progress in the continuous quality improvement cycle.

In January 1987, Motorola established its future corporate goals to be:

- Improve 100 times by 1991 (reduce the number of defects per unit to 1 percent of the existing level of defects).
- Achieve six-sigma capability by 1992 (reduce the number of defects to less than 3.4 defects per million units).

Motorola's quality improvement process is based on the pervasive use of quality improvement tools, not on the tools themselves. Success is attributed to a clear understanding by management, from the chairman on down, that if Total Customer Satisfaction (TCS) can be attained, the rest of the business will take care of itself. Most operational issues become crises only as a result of some failure to totally satisfy the internal or external customer. Concurrent with this understanding is the integration of quality strategy into the day-to-day operations.

Motorola attributes earning the Malcolm Baldrige National Quality Award to seven key items in its structure and approach to quality. Within the seven areas, the following are considered significant.

Leadership. The quality culture is pervasive and TCS is fundamental to success. Everyone in the company is responsible for customer satisfaction.

Information and analysis. The collection of information must focus on defects found, compared to the number of opportunities to make defects. Data systems record defects, opportunities, and the means, variation and limits of product and process.

Planning for quality. Long- and short-term goals focus on TCS. Strategic objectives are included in the corporate long range plan to permit managing the quality improvement objects just as new product introduction, technology, or other activities are managed.

Human resource utilization. Involvement and contribution of individuals in the TCS approach focus on providing individuals the knowledge and skills to perform at the desired level. Training in quality is deemed the key to this. In 1985, 37 percent of the training was devoted to quality; in 1986, 43 percent; and in 1987, 73 percent. In 1987, $44 million, or 2.4 percent of the corporate payroll, was spent on training. Training is devoted to quality improvement processes, principles, technology, and objectives.

Quality assurance of products and services. Motorola's senior executives visit customers to listen to the "Voice of the Customer" and provide top-down emphasis on customer requirements. The implementation and sharp focus on the quality improvement program has brought about the desired results and established new goals for which Motorola will strive.

Quality results. As a result of Motorola's quality efforts, it is alone as the non-Japanese supplier of pagers to Nippon Telegraph and Telephone. Motorola is also the only semiconductor supplier for very-high-speed integrated circuits to the Department of Defense.

Customer satisfaction. Motorola's efforts, reported by *Electronics Business* magazine, show that it has received nearly fifty quality awards and certified supplier citations, more than any other company in a 600-company survey. This number of awards and citations more than doubled in 1986.

Motorola's success is a story of dedicated flow-down of the customer's requirements and aggressive implementation of tools, practices, and techniques to achieve quality levels far exceeding expectations of the 1970s. Its efforts to provide TCS earned Motorola the Malcolm Baldrige National Quality Award.

Pharmaceutical

In one pharmaceutical company, quality management in drug development focuses on input activities to provide products, information, and services to the project's customers that conform to their requirements every time. Consistently conforming to the requirements brings about customer satisfaction while preventing problems and providing the basis for process improvement which can shorten development time [45].

Senior company management is critical to the quality management process. Their functions center around six key areas.

- Provide strategic direction for research and development efforts
- Set policy, procedure, and performance standards
- Allocate the necessary resources of time, money, and people
- Select the project leaders and provide the necessary support
- Conduct regular reviews and set priorities for the project
- Provide decisions for continuance or termination of the project at milestones

The drug development cycle may encompass a span of six to ten years with associated costs of $30 million to $60 million. The stages of development are typically:

- Drug discovery
- Animal safety evaluation
- Human safety evaluation
- Human efficacy evaluation
- Long-term human and animal safety evaluation
- Registration preparation and filing
- Market approval and launch

Drug development is a process of a series of interrelated, complex activities as it progresses through each stage. The customers change during these stages, but must be considered throughout the life cycle of the development. The prime customers for each stage are:

• Drug discovery stage	R&D management
• Animal safety evaluation	Government agencies
• Human safety evaluation	Government agencies
• Human efficacy evaluation	Government agencies
• Long-term human and animal safety evaluation	Government agencies
• Registration preparation and filing	Government agencies
• Market approval and launch	Marketing department

Although the primary customers drive many of the requirements for drug development, there are secondary and tertiary customers at each stage. Most important of all is the end product consumer, the patient. Physicians and pharmacists must also be considered in the end product customer line because of their vital role in prescribing, recommending, and monitoring the use of any marketed drug. Company management, with the inherent responsibility for overall company profitability, will always be a customer for the project leader.

In summary, quality management in the pharmaceutical industry includes rigorous adherence to the guidelines and rules established by government agencies while satisfying multiple customers with different responsibilities and interests. Within the guidelines of safety and efficacy, the project leader must "conform to the requirements" of all customers, who may have conflicting requirements. This may require negotiations and discussions with competing customers to resolve conflicts between requirements.

Construction

In February 1983, *The Business Roundtable* reported the results of its efforts in surveying the cost effectiveness of quality assurance/quality control programs in the construction industry in the United States. The objectives of the survey were to determine how effectively the industry was addressing quality assurance functions and to identify recurring problems related to quality assurance and their impact on the overall project efforts. Furthermore, the objective was to identify and evaluate opportunities to improve quality assurance efforts through corrective actions and applications of new and existing technology which would produce cost reductions in the construction process.

Major findings of the study were:

- The application and benefits of a quality assurance/quality control (QA/QC) program were neither fully understood nor effectively utilized in planning, design, and construction phases.
- Formalized QA/QC programs "evolved" rather than having been planned on a sound engineering basis.
- One-third of all companies in the study had no formal QA/QC program in design.
- One-fourth of the companies in the study had no identifiable QA/QC program in construction.
- Most companies initiated QA/QC programs because they were required to do so rather than believing that such programs would be beneficial and cost effective.
- Quality problems arose and quality procedures were initiated to prevent future recurrences.
- Most companies did not have quantitative cost data to measure effectiveness of QA/QC programs.
- Few companies used statistical methods or automatic data processing equipment in their QA/QC programs.

The results of the study describe the pre-1983 condition of the QA/QC programs in the construction industry, which at best could be characterized as extremely weak in having a viable quality orientation. The lack of interest and emphasis by senior managers and owners was evidenced by the low or non-existent QA/QC budgets in many companies, and programs mandated by law (such as the nuclear power plant construction) were ineffective, nearly always exceeding the allocated budgets. The study by The Business Roundtable highlighted the need for improvements in QA/QC programs while establishing a baseline from which companies could measure progress. In the past seven years, there have been major thrusts at improving quality while reducing the costs of projects.

Department of Defense (DoD)

The U.S. Department of Defense, in addition to other federal government agencies, has initiated a Total Quality Management (TQM) program to implement a productivity improvement program within the federal government. TQM is designed to implement policies, principles, and practices which will apply quantitative methods and human resources to improve the material and services supplied to an organization, all the processes with an organization, and the degree to which the needs of the customer are met, now and in the future. The key policy points are listed below.

a. Fundamentals of the DoD TQM policy
- A quality- and productivity-oriented defense industry with its underlying industrial base is the key to our (DoD) ability to maintain a superior level of readiness.
- Quality is absolutely vital to our defense, and requires a commitment to continuous improvement by all DoD personnel.
- Quality must be a key element of competition.

- Acquisition strategies must include requirements for continuous improvement of quality and reduced ownership costs.
- Sustained DoD-wide emphasis and concern with respect to high quality and productivity must be an integral part of our daily operations.

b. Conditions for quality
- Quality concepts must be ingrained throughout every organization with proper training at each level, starting with top management.
- Managers and personnel at all levels must take responsibility for the quality of their efforts.
- Competent, dedicated employees make the greatest contributions to quality and productivity. They must be recognized and rewarded accordingly.
- Principles of quality improvement must involve all personnel and products.

c. Approach to quality
- Technology, being one of our greatest assets, must be widely used to continuously improve the quality of defense systems, equipment, and services.
- Emphasis must change from relying on inspection, to designing and building quality into the process and product.
- Quality improvement is a key to productivity improvement and must be pursued with the necessary resources to produce tangible benefits.

In implementing the TQM policy, several actions have been taken. Two major contracts have been awarded by the Office of Personnel Management to teach the principles of TQM. Any government agency may call upon the services of the two companies providing TQM orientations to obtain in-house training programs. The cost to the government agency is defined in the contract and the money is transferred to the Office of Personnel Management to pay for the services.

In another initiative to implement the DoD TQM program, key personnel in offices and activities have been designated "TQM Facilitators" for the purpose of guiding the quality functions within their respective offices or activities. These individuals receive training in the TQM process and procedures for full implementation of quality aspects as the TQM program grows. Senior managers are appointed to recognize individual performance with "Gold Star" pins, which are worn on the outer clothing.

Most significant in the actions of DoD, because of the large amount of contracting for products and services, is the inclusion of quality requirements in contractual documentation. Major contractors are required to have an active quality program and ensure major subcontractors also have quality programs in place. These quality requirements for contracts have been codified into law and procurement regulations of the U.S. Government.

G. Summary

The world of quality is moving forward for many individuals, companies, and countries through the recognition that quality is needed to achieve productivity and the sale of products which meet the customers' requirements. The shift is toward achieving total customer satisfaction through programs which respond to those requirements and bring about products that meet the customer's expectations.

Projects are like any other process that attempts to develop a product—the correct balance of ingredients must be inserted into the process and managed to achieve the desired results. The major difference between projects and manufacturing is that projects do not replicate the processes as frequently as the manufacturing processes. There is a need, however, to tailor the manufacturing concepts for projects to capitalize on the advances achieved in quality management.

Understanding the customer is key to determining the true requirements of a project. Secondly, it is necessary to have a common basis for defining the customer's requirements. This chapter defines the categories of customers and the nine common characteristics or attributes for project definition.

Chapter II   Dimensions of Customer Requirements

A. Understanding the Customer

To be able to define and appreciate the needs of the customer, it is important to understand the types of customer and the number of customers on a project. The size and dollar value of the project does not dictate the type of customer nor does it dictate the number of customers. Projects of all sizes and dollar values have a mix of customers that are unique to that situation.

Types of Customer

There are two general categories of customers who must be served in the project environment. The first, apparent customers, such as those with an economic interest, are called the stakeholders in the project. These customers are easily identifiable and will shape the project direction, size, duration, budget, and other major physical aspects.

The second category, invisible customers, have no interest in the project meeting its goals, but are customers in the sense that they attempt to shape the project to meet their individual interests. Examples of the invisible customers are environmentalists who want the project canceled, changed, or delayed; trade unions that want to serve its membership by compartmenting types of work for different craftspersons; and government agencies that issue regulations or directives which affect the planned progress of the project. Both categories of customers must be served to ensure project success.

Number of Customers

Contrary to popular opinion, a project seldom has a single customer. The customer in the traditional sense is the owner or buyer of the product or services while all other participants are assumed to have other roles. In fact, the listing of all apparent and invisible customers will clarify the issue as to the number of customers when a single entity is buying the product or services. On the other hand, however, there can be multiple customers who may be placed in the buyers category.

For example, there is a hospital being built in Texas that is typical of the multiple customer situation. The hospital is being purchased by an affiliation of physicians for use by several departments of medicine. Each department is headed by a physician who has requirements for space to provide health care services and house the associated equipment. The physicians are the multiple customers for the contractor (project manager) to satisfy in allotting space and accommodating the physicians. Because the physicians (customers) were not included in the original planning, the specifications were not developed around their requirements and the situation developed into a negotiated trade-off of space between competing space requirements.

The customers of the project and their interests in the project should be identified during the conceptual phase of a project to determine the actions required to meet each one's requirements. A sample of project customers is shown in Figure II.1.

CUSTOMER	TYPE	INTEREST IN PROJECT
Buyer/Owner	Apparent	−financial interest
Sponsor/Financier	Apparent	−financial interest
Public at Large	Invisible	−ecology, public safety, aesthetic
Seller/Contractor	Apparent	−financial interest
Project Team	Apparent	−professional, financial
Government Agency	Invisible	−public interests

Figure II.1. Project Customers (Example)

B. Defining The Buyer's (Customer's) Requirements

The buyer's (customer's) desires may well be stated in extremely simple terms that imply a range of options which will satisfy the requirement. On the other hand, the desire may be stated in explicit terms that leave little or no latitude in translating the desire to a final product. Both situations have their shortcomings.

The customer's desires stated in simple terms may not meet the requirement in that the customer has not fully thought through the request. Therefore, a simple statement of "I want a hotel with 240 rooms" could be met in a number of ways. A ten-story building with 24 rooms per floor, a one-story building with 240 rooms, a 240-room hotel with all rooms of similar design, or a 240-room hotel with a different design for each room would meet this simple request. It is reasonable to assume that none of these basic configurations would meet the customer's real requirements.

The customer's desire stated in explicit, detailed terms would probably be as difficult to satisfy as the simple statement of requirements. When a customer is so specific in defining the requirement, the details are often flawed. The customer must, as a minimum, have sufficient knowledge of the process to assure safety, design integrity, materials, and work methods. Overly detailed requirements that dictate how the work will be accomplished is one of the major weaknesses in the specification system of the U.S. Government.

It is best to work with the customer to determine the requirements in terms both parties understand and agree to the meanings. One federal agency conducts a "mutual understanding conference" before a contract is signed to ensure that the requirements of the contract are understood and the performing contractor will meet those requirements. Failure to understand the requirements from the onset of the project will impede planning, implementation/execution, maintenance/operation, and delivery of the system.

C. Project Characteristics/Attributes

A project or the system of the project possesses characteristics and attributes that describe the form, fit, and function. One set of characteristics and attributes is called the *'ilities*. Performance of a product is often described in terms of the "Nine *'ilities*." These *'ilities* may be used to most accurately describe the needs of the customer and are fully described in the specification process of codifying a product prior to the build phase. A balance of these *'ilities* makes the quality of the product as seen through the customer's eyes.

The assessment of products is often formally evaluated and compared in the area of the *'ilities*. The *'ilities* most accurately describe the utility of a product for the consumer and establish a basis for evaluating the value of that product when making financial comparisons. Definitions of the *'ilities* follow.

Producibility

Producibility (called constructibility in the construction industry) is the ability of a product or service to be produced within the existing technology, human resource skills and knowledge, and materials at a cost compatible with the market expectations and within the scope of societal values. Producibility may depend upon certain processes that deal with new materials such as composites or special manufacturing techniques. Producibility is one of the most critical aspects of developing any new product.

Usability

Usability is the ability of a product to perform its intended function for the specified user under the prescribed conditions. The combination of performance, function, and condition are the keys to defining the usability of a product. Changing one or more of these parameters may adversely affect the others to a significant degree. For example, the use of a knife as a screwdriver may perform the desired function, but will surely reduce performance for the intended life of the knife. The usability function is often considered in the human engineering design to assure the product meets the ergonomic criteria for use.

Reliability

Reliability is the degree to which a unit of equipment performs its intended function under specified conditions for a specified period of time. Reliability is usually specified as Mean Time Between Failure, or MTBF. Reliability is computed by two methods and the results have different meanings: predicted and actual.

Predicted MTBF is based on a mathematical computation of part or component failure using a "tree diagram" to determine sequential failure aspects of the part or component rated periods. The predicted MTBF is least desirable because it cannot account for environmental variations that can degrade components to lower rates.

Actual MTBF is the use of "field collected" data to compute the failures under realistic operating conditions to find the average (mean) time between failure. This actual reliability will seldom be the same as the predicted reliability.

Maintainability

Maintainability is the ability of a unit to be restored within a specified time to its performance capability under the environmental operating conditions within a specified, average period of time. Maintainability is usually stated in Mean Time To Repair, or MTTR, for the average time to make minor repairs and would not include major repairs of the unit or detailed repair of some components.

MTTR is based on a maintenance philosophy that specifies which types of repair will be accomplished at each level, where these levels may be: operator repair, shop repair, and rebuild. The maintenance philosophy, for example, may specify the operator repair to be less than one hour MTTR for all work authorized to be performed. The shop repair may specify less than three hours MTTR for all work authorized to be performed. The rebuild would not necessarily be specified as MTTR, but specified as hours to perform major overhaul functions.

The quantity of authorized repair at each level and the time to repair the equipment is a function of the totality of maintaining a piece of equipment. The stock level for repair parts and the requisite human resource skills and knowledge are a part of the overall maintenance philosophy.

Availability

Availability is the probability of a product being capable of performing a required function under the specified conditions when called upon. The two key parts of availability are Reliability and Maintainability. The combination of MTBF, or the average time of operation between repairs, and MTTR, the average time to repair any malfunctioning component, directly affects the availability of a given piece of equipment. In some work environments, reliability, maintainability, and availability are treated as a single design function because of their interrelationship.

Operability

Operability is the ability of a product to be operated by human resources (often specified in percentiles) for specified periods of time under given conditions without significant degradation of the output. As an example, a farmer must be able to maneuver a tractor through the fields for as many as twelve hours in a day without serious fatigue or imposing a safety hazard to himself or others.

Flexibility

Flexibility is the ability of a product to be used for different purposes, at different capacities, and under different conditions. Most products are specified single-purpose, dual-purpose, or multi-purpose and designed to meet those requirements. When a product is found to have a "hidden" function for which it was not designed, the product may suffer from reduced reliability because it is being stressed beyond its design limits. Flexibility may add value to a product and enhance its sale, but with subsequent loss of sale because it does not meet new perceptions of reliability.

Many products are designed for a single purpose and are not intended to be used for more than one function. It can be seen, however, that a multi-purpose product, such as a hand tool, would have greater value to the consumer than a single purpose hand tool. This same concept is applicable to buildings that can be used for multiple purposes such as a garage, a warehouse, or a factory.

Social Acceptability

Social acceptability is the degree of compatibility between the characteristics of a product or service and the prevailing values and expectations of the relevant society; and the degree to which the public accepts a product for use. The acceptability of a product may range from tangible to intangible areas for acceptance or rejection of a product. The social acceptability usually is the perceived function or dysfunction of a product, and may not have any bearing on the actual product characteristics.

Major factors in this area are safety, environmental impact, and appearance. Any product or service with an actual or perceived safety defect will suffer reduced sales. Similar to the product or service, the project process must be acceptable. A process that creates an odor which pervades the community will often cause rejection of the end product. Soap, for example, may present a pleasant odor as an end product, but the odor in the manufacturing process could easily alienate a large number of potential customers.

There are many examples of the public rejecting a product or taking some action against companies because of negative publicity concerning the product. For illustrative purposes, a few examples follow.

- A building can be rejected because it resembles something distasteful. In Vienna, Virginia, there are two buildings that illustrate the concept, one has a facade that resembles a toilet seat while the other has a design that resembles a shopping bag. Few people will visit the "Toilet Seat" or the "Brick Shopping Bag" to conduct business. The businesses of the buildings do not seem to have stability, and new businesses frequently replace them.
- The Ford Pinto with the gasoline tank that exploded when struck from the rear created some negative feelings toward the product. The General Motors Chevette was also reported to have a gasoline tank that would not withstand

an impact from the rear without rupturing and spilling gasoline. The Audi with the automatic transmission that was reported to accelerate without pressure on the gas pedal gave cause for concern when it was alleged that the condition was the proximate cause of several injuries and deaths.

- The continual emphasis on protecting the environment from hazardous products or by-products has been highlighted in the news media. Chemical plants have been called to account for "dumping" hazardous waste materials in rivers, streams, and lakes. Nuclear waste is another by-product that must be disposed of through safe means while protecting the environment.
- The oil tanker, Exxon Valdez, ran aground and ruptured the oil tanks which allowed crude oil to spill into Prince William Sound off the coast of Alaska. This situation received adverse publicity and major efforts were made by environmentalists to force the Exxon Oil Company to recover the polluting substance from the beaches, animals, and waters. The Exxon Valdez was renamed the Exxon Mediterranean to avoid the stigma of the oil spill.

Affordability

Affordability is the ability to develop, acquire, operate, maintain, and dispose of a product over its life. The cost of each phase of ownership has a different value based on such items as design, manufacture, maintainability, reliability, and use. There must be a balance between the initial cost of a product and the operation and maintenance costs.

For example, an automobile with an initial cost of $100,000 could not sell many units even though the operation and maintenance costs might be as low as one cent per mile. (Normal operation and maintenance costs range between 25 and 45 cents.) Similarly, if the initial cost was $2,000 and the operation and maintenance costs were $2.10 per mile, the cost of ownership is still out of proportion with current standards (and expectations). The initial acquisition cost as well as the operation and maintenance costs are critical to the customer.

Affordability may be viewed in the classic model as being 10 percent cost for development, 30 percent cost of purchase, and 60 percent cost for operation and maintenance. This classic model shows a relatively low cost for development, e.g., design, test, fix, while the major portion of the cost is in the operation and maintenance. A shift of more of the cost to design, for example, may easily reduce operation and maintenance costs for a net overall savings during the life of a product. An example of this increased allocation of resources to the design phase design is the Boeing 757 aircraft that, through improved design, reduced the number of crew members in the cockpit from a normal crew of five to only three. The additional design cost eliminated the costs for two crew members during the entire operation phase of the aircraft.

The 'ilities give a framework for converting the customer's requirements into specifications with finite measures for the characteristics and attributes of the product or service. The specification establishes the means to communicate the product or service parameters to designers and constructors as well as providing feedback to the customers. Furthermore, the specification parameters establish the baseline for testing, change control/configuration management, and any subsequent product or service improvement.

D. Specification Practices

From a quality perspective, it is important to understand the types of specifications and specification practices being used to describe the customer's requirements. The form of specification used can easily permit variances from the customer's expectations and a subsequent failure to meet the end requirement.

Functional Specification

In this type of specification, the focus is on the functions that the product will provide over its useful period of operation. The terminology relates to the type of functions that the product is to achieve.

An example of a functional specification for a telephone could be: Deliver two devices that permits voice communication when connected by two copper wires. The device shall permit intelligible information to be transmitted and received over a distance of 500 feet, weigh not more than 8 ounces, require no external power source, and be capable of simultaneous listen and talk communication functions.

The functional specification provides the seller a wide latitude in acquiring, developing, or building the product. The parametric values are not specified and the functions may be described in general terms that are subject to interpretation by both the buyer and seller. Functional specifications, of course, must be converted into values that can be used to positively define the requirement of the customer.

Detailed Specification

A detailed specification is one that uses parametric values to describe the requirement. This specification may be developed by the customer or may be one jointly developed by the customer and the seller. This document is very precise in its description of the product.

An example of a detailed specification could be: Construct one kitchen table using all maple wood and glue that measures 40 x 40 inches on the surface and is 28 inches high. The table shall be one solid piece after integration of the wood surface and legs. The finish shall be smooth to the touch before applying a varnish coat and three subsequent coats. When complete, the table shall be capable of supporting 120 pounds of weight on the top side when the weight is evenly distributed at not less than four points. The table finish shall be resistant to dents, scarring, or scratching under normal use.

The detailed specification becomes involved in the size, functions, and assembly of the product to the level of detail desired by the customer. Materials, integration methods, skill levels of workers, size of product, and durability of the product may be precisely stated by the customer. This precision permits the seller to meet the customer's requirements more easily than the functional specification because the customer's expectations are known in detail.

E. Summary

The ability to meet the customer's requirements depends upon an understanding of the range of practices for describing a product. The type of customer, the number of customers, and the understanding of the characteristics and attributes of a product are essential to describing products for a mutual understanding of the requirements. The form of describing the requirements also materially affects the outcome for integrating or building a product. For a project, the correct combination of the product's attributes and characteristics to describe the customer's requirements provides the baseline for a quality product. Subsequent communications regarding the project are facilitated because of the mutual understanding from the onset of the work.

Planning a project requires an understanding of the needs of individuals, elements of a project plan, supporting plans, test requirements, and the project as a process. Viewing and planning a project as a process gives new insight into techniques to achieve a quality orientation during the early stage of a project. A review of some lessons learned in planning and difficulty in implementing plans promotes understanding of the requirements and areas to avoid.

Chapter III   Planning for Quality in Projects

A. Planning

Planning implies the ability to anticipate situations and prepare actions that will bring about the desired outcome. This is typically accomplished through the development of broad objectives, which are divided in a tree-like fashion to develop lower level goals. These lower level goals are translated into actions within an operational framework and the proper resources are assigned in a plan to perform the actions. Project managers, of course, have the responsibility to ensure these actions are planned, documented, and implemented in the sequence which will bring about customer satisfaction by meeting the customer's requirements and expectations.

Planning also entails communicating the correct actions in a form which is understandable and complete. Because the requirements for quality must be integrated into the project plan, it is necessary to examine the project as it is defined and the product which it is to deliver. Both planning knowledge and planning skills are essential to the development of a comprehensive project plan that ensures the customer is satisfied with the end result.

B. Project Manager's Needs

In planning projects, it is essential that planners bring out critical project characteristics so that the project manager may direct the work toward completion. There is a need to describe key elements which directly contribute to meeting the customer's requirements. This can be accomplished when criteria for project planning are established and implemented.

The criteria for project managers encompass four areas which must be considered during planning and the plan must include the provisions to support these actions.

Visualize. Project managers must be able to clearly visualize the project relationships among tasks and identify the critical tasks. The planning of the tasks and all supporting documentation must make the tasks and relationships visible. In this manner, project managers may focus their attention on the work.

Calculate. Project managers must be able to immediately calculate the effects of changes in the project and initiate any appropriate corrective action to maintain the momentum while continuing to meet the customer's requirements. Plans, therefore, must contain sufficient detail to determine the affected actions. This will give the project manager the information with which to calculate a new course of action.

Decide. Project managers must decide how to make the most effective use of all resources. Plans such as budgets, schedules, and implementation guidelines are means of assigning resources to tasks to ensure the project makes the best use of each allocated resource. The decision to assign resources also includes the allocation of the proper amount to meet the quality requirements.

Communicate. Project managers must effectively communicate to others what is necessary to complete tasks on time and to specifications. The communication of requirements must be clear and unambiguous. Thorough planning of the project and documenting of the detailed requirements permits effective communication of the project's needs.

C. Key Elements in Project Planning

In planning for quality management of a project, certain elements are considered essential to conducting the total project work and focusing on the customer's requirements.

Initial Planning

Initial planning of the overall project must, as a minimum, include the following areas.

Network planning. The logical sequence of work accomplishment through a structured plan.

Time analysis. The capability for comparison of planned and actual time durations.

Resource analysis. The capability for comparison of planned and actual resources committed to the project.

Cost analysis. The capability for comparison of planned and actual costs for the project's activities.

Multiple schedules. The development of "what-if," or contingency, schedules for alternative courses of action.

Progress reporting. The routine reporting of the status of the project as compared to the planned progress. This includes variances from the plan for time, cost, and technical performance status.

Reports and charts/plots. The graphic summaries of the status of the project, depicted in a comparative manner.

Key events. The key events, or those the customer believes to be important to reflect the status of the project. In addition, the project manager may have key events that are used to the control the project.

Earliest dates/deadlines/activity logic. The earliest and latest start dates for all activities to include the logical association between activities.

The Secondary Items

The secondary items in planning a project are often forgotten because they do not have an impact on the initiation of the project's work. These are, however, extremely important areas for planning.

Upgrade drawings/incorporate changes. The policies and procedures to ensure any changes to the configuration of the project's product are included in the documentation. This is important to know how the project's product has been changed for final product descriptions as well as monitoring the change to the scope of work during implementation.

Producibility/constructibility review. The scheduling of a critical review of the design of the product to ensure the end product can be built in its final form. This review should be held prior to the commitment to the final product and is based on a technical assessment of the design, technology, skills available, and other factors affecting the actual build phase.

Testability review. The scheduling of a review of the ability to conduct a meaningful test or demonstration of the product's capabilities. Test criteria to demonstrate technical performance should be developed prior to contract award to ensure mutual agreement between the customer and the project manager.

Acceptance requirements documents review. The scheduling of a review of the acceptance criteria documentation to ensure mutual agreement between the customer and the project manager. The acceptance criteria should be a part of the contract, but may be in general form. The detail acceptance criteria may be further defined in a requirements document.

Procurement plan. The procedures for purchasing materials, equipment, and services for the project. This plan can include approved vendors and subcontractors as well as defining the acceptance criteria for materials. It will also cover "make-buy" decisions, long-lead items, vendor quotes, and vendor selections.

Types of Plans

Traditionally, project planning has been a hierarchy of documents with many of the functional areas included in a separate document. The division of the functional areas into separate plans is efficient for the planning process, but has major drawbacks in implementation. For example, the quality plan is often kept in the quality manager's office and assumed by others to be only for the quality personnel. The quality plan, however, is a integral part of the overall implementation and must be available to all parties.

Some of the types of plans currently in use that should be integrated into the project plan are list below.

Program quality requirement plan. The document that describes the quality requirements and processes or procedures to be used to meet the customer's product requirements. This document will usually cite corporate and industry standards to be used to meet the specific parameters of the product.

Facilities plan. The document that describes the temporary or permanent facilities and their uses during a project's implementation. It will also specify whether the facilities are to be a part of the project product after use by the project team or if they are to be removed.

Manufacturing plan. The document that describes the processes, procedures, and methods for building a product. This plan will include sufficient detail to provide guidance in any build phase of a project.

Implementation plan. This document describes how the project will be executed or conducted, and will describe the major components and assemblies to be installed. It will usually include the initial schedule and budget for the project as well as specific instructions for the sequential building of the project.

System sell-off plan. The document that describes how the product will be delivered to the customer and the customer's acceptance procedures. It may include procedures for demonstrating the functions and operating characteristics of the product.

System test plan. The document that describes the number and types of tests to be conducted to ensure the product meets the requirement. It states the parametric criteria that a product must meet and when the tests will be conducted.

Configuration management plan. The document that describes the policies and procedures for establishing a baseline of the product design and the means for changing the design. It will list the criteria for changes and the approving authorities for levels of change.

Test Philosophy

Testing or demonstrating to the customer the capabilities of the product is important to showing that the customer's requirements have been met. This visible demonstration of the capabilities provides the customer confidence in the product and assures all performance criteria have been met. Therefore, the planning must include test or demonstration of the capabilities and the test philosophy in anticipation of the requirements.

Test philosophies depend upon the complexity of the product, the degree to which testing can be accomplished at various points in the build phase, the maturity of the technology used, and the cost of testing. One test philosophy for a complex device being built in a job shop mode used the following approach.

- Build components and test.
- Integrate components and test.
- Test after each successive build or integration to reduce the chance of failure in the end product, reducing the potential for tear-down costs to replace items, but increasing fabrication costs.

The end result is a quality product that has been through several successive function or capability tests at each stage of the build.

The rationale for the above test philosophy was that a long assembly line requires 100 percent testing. It is easier to test more frequently than to perform the repair and rework. Also, 100 percent vendor acceptance testing was less costly than identifying bad parts during the assembly process.

D. The Anatomy of a Project

Projects take on several different meanings, and all can be logical from the different perspectives of the owner, contractor, project manager, project team or other participants. One may define a project in terms that fit a particular industry, discipline, field, or vocation. To understand quality management in a project, it is helpful to review the project's internal functions and the alternatives for the project's composition.

Over the past twenty years, the description of a project has evolved to imply a single, dedicated effort to produce a system, product, or service. Other interpretations and definitions lead to a more general statement regarding the project's definition.

Projects are temporary, goal-oriented efforts that produce a product or service for delivery to a customer. The time-constrained nature of the project dictates a rapid assembly of personnel with the correct skills and knowledge to convert raw materials, components, parts, assemblies, and pieces into a product that conforms to the customer's requirements. The project can be viewed as an integration effort where the project manager melds together the correct blend of personnel, materials, processes, and procedures.

The definition adopted by the Project Management Institute to communicate the concept of a project was developed by practitioners, professors, students, and managers actively engaged in the project management profession. The definition in the Project Management Body of Knowledge (PMBOK) focuses on the time and resource constraints of the project [155].

Project: Any undertaking with a defined starting point and defined objectives by which completion is identified. In practice, most projects depend on finite or limited resources by which the objectives are to be accomplished.

The first definition involves quality in that "the product conforms to the customer's requirements" while the PMBOK definition is a more general state-

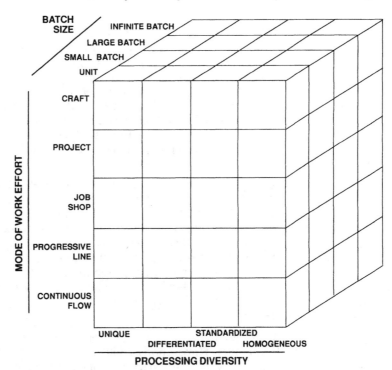

Figure III.1. Process Matrix

ment about time and resources to accomplish the objectives. Any definition of a project must include time, cost (of resources), and quality (product satisfaction of the customer's requirements). The increased emphasis within the business community to obtain "total customer satisfaction" almost dictates that quality become the "first among equals" in the time-cost-quality triad.

A Classification of Work Efforts

An important aspect of project definition is a list of concepts by which it can be described. Although the existing literature discloses several classifications, none mention project as a distinctive concept [53] [104] [142]. Work efforts are listed, however, which are typically performed in the project mode. Thus, a classification is required to promote understanding of the project.

A classification was developed that has three dimensions—mode of work effort, batch size, and diversity of processing—to form a "process matrix." This process matrix is depicted in Figure III-1[138][139].

a. **Modes of work effort.** There are five basic modes in which work is accomplished. While most organizations perform some work in several of these modes, generally one mode is dominant in the core technology of the organization or project. Technology in this sense does not imply just engineering or manufacturing technologies but includes all sorts of office technologies, including the copier as well as the computer, and the technologies involved in producing an advertising or political campaign, designing a training program or a curriculum, or producing a movie.

The five modes of work effort are:

Craft. A process composed of a combination of one or more technologies/operations involving homogeneous human resources, generally a single person, producing a narrow range of products/services. This is best characterized by the single artist/craftsperson producing one unit of product at a time. Other examples are of a single cook preparing a meal to order or a doctor examining a patient in the doctor's office.

Project. A temporary process composed of an unique mix of technologies/operations involving the close coordination of heterogeneous resources to produce one or a few units of a unique product/service.

Job shop. A process composed of a loosely coordinated collection of heterogeneous technologies/operations to create a wide range of products/services where the technologies are located in groups by function and the time required at each work station is varied. This is best characterized by the manufacturing plant in which equipment is located or grouped into departments by type or function and the product/service is performed by moving the unit being worked upon from one department to another in a non-uniform manner. It is also the mode of operation of many kitchens and the mode used for physical examinations performed in hospitals.

Progressive line. A process composed of a tightly coordinated collection of heterogeneous technologies/operations to produce a limited range of products/services in which the technologies are serially located, the operator is directly involved in the work on the product, and the time allotted at each work station is the same. The automotive assembly line is the stereotypical example. Since this mode is used for both assembly and disassembly, the general term, "progressive," is more appropriate. It is also the typical mode of serving for cafeterias and the mode in which physical examinations are given to large groups of people, such as for the military. Manufacturing cells also fit in this category.

Continuous flow. A process composed of a tightly coordinated collection of technologies/operations which are uniformly applied over time and to all the many units of a very narrow range of products/services, and in which the role of the operator is primarily to monitor and adjust the processes. Petroleum refineries are the most popular example of this mode. Electric generating stations, water and sewage treatment facilities, and automatic transfer lines such as those used in producing engine blocks and transmission housings are also included in this mode.

b. **Batch size.** Another identified variable is batch size. Batch size can be divided into four classes:

Unit. One-off as is generally the case in projects, often the case in some job shops, and frequently in the craft mode.

Small. Occurs occasionally in projects, but most frequently in job shop and craft modes.

Large. Most likely to occur in job shops and progressive line, but is often used in producing chemical products in continuous flow mode.

Infinite. Typical of refineries, chemical plants, and utilities.

c. **Diversity in processing.** One other characteristic of processes which provides insight into applicable techniques, procedures, and practices is diversity in processing. Diversity in processing is categorized as:

Unique. Every unit receives different processing. This is frequent in the craft and project modes and often in the job shop mode. A van customizing shop may operate in this manner with each unit being designed, built and trimmed differently.

Differentiated. Many processes are standardized but non-standard processing is allowed on certain features.

Standardized. Each process is designed to include two or more options. Each unit receives processing according to one of these options at each processing step. No deviations are allowed from these standard processes although the combination of options can lead to millions of unique products.

Homogeneous. Every unit receives exactly the same treatment, such as in a petroleum refinery where a unit might be considered a gallon of hydrocarbon. This characteristic, however, is not unique to continuous flow mode.

These three process characteristics—mode of work, batch size, and process type—form the process matrix. Projects tend to produce single or a few units but occasionally produce a considerable quantity of units as a part of the project. Most products of projects are unique but some are simply differentiated or even standardized. For example, one housing project produced 740 units of some ten standardized designs.

E. The Project or the Product of the Project

The word "project" is often ambiguously used, sometimes referring to the project and sometimes referring to the product of the project. This is not a trivial distinction as both entities have characteristics unique unto themselves. The names of some of these characteristics apply to both. For example, the life cycle cost of a product includes the cost of creating it (a project), the cost of operating it, the cost of major repairs or refurbishing (typically done as a project), and the cost of dismantling (often a project, if done). A project creating a product is generally a relatively small proportion of the life cycle cost of the product.

The project should be defined to show that it is a process involving one or more modes of work, one or more batch sizes, using one or more types of process. The project could easily be one of each for the duration of the work, but more likely is a combination of more than one from each category. Thus, the framing of the project as a process with a series of subprocesses that are combinations of the categories would describe the project and facilitate the evaluation of opportunities for quality applications.

The product should be defined in the specification, statement of work, and any data requirements list. This provides a description using form, fit, function, and the characteristics shown in Chapter II.

F. The Project as a Process

Given that a project is a temporary process to produce one or a few units of a unique product/service, it is appropriate to examine the characteristics of the process.

The essential characteristic of the process by which a project is performed is the progressive elaboration of the requirements.

A project is initiated by a person (perhaps a member of an organization) recognizing a problem or opportunity about which some action is to be taken. That person, alone or in concert, develops an initial concept of the action to be taken in the form of a product, be it a product for sale, a new facility, or an advertising campaign. Much work needs to be accomplished to take this meager concept to the reality of the product. This work, though often not conceived as such, is accomplished by instituting a project.

The initiation of a project, when viewed as a process using a combination of the "mode of work," "batch size," and "process type," takes on a new dimension for the planner. Rather than planning from start to finish for the project, the process is planned in reverse. The end product is described in a time domain of the future that is the result of the requirements of the customer. The end product is divided into components to determine what is the desired input to achieve the end product. Successive division and assignment of inputs is continued until the project is at its start point. This concept is shown in Figure III.2.

G. The Dimensions of Projects

The project environment is dynamic and presents special challenges to individuals attempting to implement new concepts. A project is by its very nature a challenge to conceptualize, plan, implement, and close out within the traditional triad of Cost-Schedule-Quality. A project has goals for all aspects of

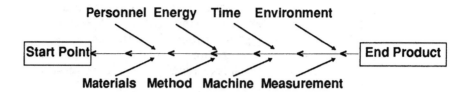

The eight resources are:

- **Personnel.** The human resources with the requisite skills and knowledge to perform functions that build the project's product or perform the project's services.
- **Energy.** The source of power (e.g., electricity, gasoline, nuclear fission, steam) to provide the project a means to operate machinery which will integrate parts, divide materials, or change the shape of materials.
- **Time.** The continuum in which work is performed in a structured succession. It is a medium which must be allotted to permit a duration for the logical conduct of activities.
- **Environment.** The project's work location and surrounding area which can be described by the weather, climate, temperature, and other natural and man-made elements that influence the project's progress.
- **Materials.** The consumable substances that comprise a project and may be installed as components or as changed items to form a part, component, or assembly of a large element.
- **Method.** The processes or procedures for accomplishing work to achieve the desired results.
- **Machine.** Any tool, implement, instrument, or vehicle which is used to perform the project's tasks.
- **Measurement.** The practice of establishing standards for gauging elements of the project to determine whether they meet the requirements; also, the maintenance of the calibration standards for the measuring devices.

Figure III.2.   Product to Initiation Planning Flow

the triad and each is considered important to the successful achievement of the end product or service being delivered to the customer.

The project is defined in both inclusive and exclusive terms. Inclusive terms tell what **is** to be accomplished in the project's work or scope, and is usually described through cost, schedule, and quality factors. Exclusive terms tell what **is not** to be included in the project's work or scope. An example of the use of inclusive and exclusive terms in one sentence is: Complete all landscaping of the property similar to adjacent property (inclusive), but leave any existing trees on the property (exclusive).

Cost

Project cost is one of the standard measures of success. It alone has considerable impact on the perceptions of success or failure of a project and is one of the first measures viewed by senior management.

Schedule

The schedule, or time duration, of a project is another measure of project success and in itself is a critical aspect of meeting the customer's needs for a product or service at a given time. Delivery of a product or service at a late date may significantly diminish its value.

Quality

The quality of a product or service in terms of meeting requirements/specifications is the value provided to the customer within the time specified for the price paid. The requirements/specifications are a combination of attributes and characteristics that describe the product or service in concrete and precise terms.

The composition of the attributes to provide a "quality" product or service is discussed in subsequent chapters of this book.

H. Quality Planning Lessons

Planning for quality in a project encompasses both internal and external actions, or activities, performed by individuals not under the direct control of the project manager. The project manager, however, must extend the planning to the external areas to ensure successful accomplishment of functions that could impact the project. Examples of deviations from the requirements are useful in focusing attention on both internal and external areas that have been historically weak in project planning and implementation.

The most significant impacts on the quality in a project begin during the conceptual phase. This is the time when specifications, statements of work, contractual agreements, and initial design are developed. Initial planning has the greatest impact on a project because it requires the commitment of processes, resources, schedules, and budgets. A small error that is allowed to stay in the plan is magnified several times through subsequent documents that are second or third tier in the hierarchy.

When a master plan is conceived and published, it becomes the umbrella for all lower level planning and actions. The lower tier documents reflect the ideas incorporated in the senior document. These concepts can lead to major deviations from the requirement and are costly to correct after work has started.

Conceptual Phase Lessons

Planning activities in four critical areas during the conceptual phase have had a material impact on the project's progress and the eventual product's capability to provide customer satisfaction.

Customer-project manager dialogue. There is a need to establish and maintain a dialogue with the customer to fully define the requirements of the project. This dialogue has major implications to ensure the accuracy of specifications, drawings, and other design-related documentation to meet customer expectations. The resolution of differences between the requirement and the designs to build the product must be accomplished prior to starting project implementation. Once work has started, it is difficult to change the course of events without major re-planning. Working with the customer to determine and agree to the full scope of the requirements will facilitate the implementation and smooth the course of work.

Project objectives. The project objectives must be sufficiently defined to provide a sharp focus on the work to be accomplished. Any shortfall in definition of objectives may let the project or work drift to the more convenient objectives developed or perceived by individuals involved in the work. A complete description of the project and end product provides that sharp focus on the work that is necessary to meet the objectives.

Schedule realism. Schedules must be realistic from the standpoint of the scope of work, resources, and external factors affecting the project. There is often optimism in the time duration that it will require to accomplish the work. By nature, individuals tend to be overly optimistic in the amount of work that can be accomplished in a specified period of time. This optimism over what can be realistically done will be in the range of 10 to 20 percent, depending upon the experience level of the estimator and the depth of understanding of the work to be accomplished. A realistic schedule is the basis for commitments to the customer.

Project scope. The project scope must be adequately defined to permit effective management of the required resources to meet the customer's requirements.

When the scope is defined at a high level with the idea that all work will subsequently fit under broad statements, there is a temptation to change the lower level of work to meet "new" desires of someone involved in the project. This action, if allowed to continue, will result in cost and schedule overruns that were not anticipated. Project scope should be fully defined through objectives, subobjectives, and down to the task level to ensure a complete understanding of the work required.

Implementation Phase Lessons

The implementation phase of the project is also a time for attention to quality aspects. When several areas are managed at one time and there is no plan for the work to be accomplished, the project manager can become overwhelmed with decisions as to priorities, methods of accomplishing work, or resources to be used. There is always more work to be accomplished than can be effectively managed in this situation. Managers may lose sight of key aspects of the project and deviate from the requirements. Some critical areas that are often overlooked in planning are listed below.

Team-building. There is a continual need for team-building and focus on the quality aspects of the project. This can be accomplished through the use of the parent company's policies and procedures to flow down the requirements to the project. Using a personnel skill matrix to select the proper skills and knowledge provides the project with qualified skill sets. The team, however, must be motivated through knowledge of being part of a worthwhile effort to build a quality end product. This must be communicated to the team and reinforced periodically to maintain enthusiasm and motivation.

Engineering. Engineering designs must meet the customer's requirements at the start of project implementation. Engineering weaknesses can adversely impact the quality of design to an extent that marginal changes can easily increase costs beyond the budget. Some areas deemed critical to the proper design of a product are proper interface specifications, no over- or under-design of the product, explicit design and material specifications, and grades of material specified in documentation. It is often helpful to review the design with the customer prior to initiation of work to ensure a mutual understanding of the build process.

Interfaces. Interface specification documents serve to ensure the physical, functional, electrical, data, hydraulic, and other types of interfaces. The accurate descriptions of these interfaces are essential to the assembly of components, parts, and pieces, or the interaction with external equipments or systems. One example of improperly specified interfaces is characterized by the construction of a printed circuit card where the 256 output channels were specified as "start with one and continue through all channels." The computer scientist labeled his card as "0 through 255" and the electrical engineer labeled the system as "1 through 256." All channels were offset by one.

Over-design. Over-design of a product does not add value, but does add cost to the building process. The addition of material of higher grade than required only increases the cost. For example, finished lumber that is covered with wallboard only adds to the cost because the finished material costs more. Using a significantly higher grade of solder to build an electronic device only increases the cost. Building a product to a standard specification that requires an expensive process, when a less costly process would be adequate, adds to the cost.

Under-design. When designing a product to meet the performance requirement, specifications are often lessened if it appears the schedule will be impacted. This may occur during the design process or an attempt made during the implementation phase to decrease the specified parameters to meet schedule milestones. There is always the push to seek more attractive alternatives when the schedule is tight; revising the performance standard is one of the first alternatives. A product meets the customer's requirements when the specification practices are adequate to ensure that performance is proper.

Specification practices. During the design phase, it may be convenient to use such phrases as "generally accepted engineering practices" or "a grade sufficient to meet the minimum stress requirements" to ensure the design process is not slowing the project. The lack of specificity leaves the precise definition of these terms to the reader. The problem is that the required material or process is passed to a person who does not normally possess the knowledge to meet the design requirements. This leads to deviation from the requirement, or nonconformance.

Grade of materials. All materials should be specified during the design phase and the specification should be precise in the grade of material for each process or subprocess. When the specification does not contain the precise material grade, this is left to the purchasing agent's discretion. The purchasing agent's job is to save money on all orders, which may result in lower grade material being ordered and delivered. As a minimum, the purchasing agent will be required to coordinate with the design engineer to determine the proper grade.

Procurement Lessons

Procurement activities must be considered in the quality function. The purchasing agent plays an important role in determining the grade of material or specifications of components from vendors or other suppliers. The common weaknesses found in the procurement process result from a combination of situations.

Price versus grade. The purchasing agent's responsibilities include the acquisition of materials at the lowest price to meet the scheduled delivery date. Often the grade or type of materials are not specifically defined and the purchasing agent is given the task with the only criterion: "buy the correct quantity at the lowest price." The practice of being specific in the type, grade, and quantity of materials when requesting procurement actions will ensure the requirement is properly stated.

Order and lead time. The need to allow sufficient order and lead time when requesting materials is not fully appreciated by all project participants. The purchasing agent will need a minimum amount of time to conduct the normal requisitioning process. Late orders for materials by the consumer leads to a compressed activity that increases the workload at the expense of other activities, although the increase in workload cannot ensure the material will be delivered in time to meet the project schedule. Anticipating the requirement for materials and placing orders early on will preclude project disruption.

Follow-up and delays. Orders for materials from vendors are often forgotten once the orders are placed. This leads to late deliveries and the potential for schedule impact. There is a need to periodically follow-up on orders and report any delay to the consumers. In this manner, the consumers are aware of the situation and may be able to work around the delayed material delivery.

Solicitation Process Lessons

The bidding process is intended to convey information to potential contractors for their assessment and response with a valid bid. This process is often flawed through oversight of key and essential items by both the buyer and seller. The majority of weaknesses center around three items.

Contractor qualifications. The contractor's qualifications may be less than required for the project. This occurs when the buyer does not specifically require the contractor to have experience in the type of work being bid. Also, the contractor may overstate company qualifications or state qualifications in the bid which the company no longer possesses.

Bid package review. The review of the bid package by the contractor (seller) and the owner (buyer) is frequently considered unimportant to the understanding and communication of requirements and is often overlooked. Casual or cursory review can easily lead to misunderstandings and contract disputes. A review should always be made prior to contract signing to assure a mutual understanding of the requirements and of the contractor's capability to perform to that level.

Contractor's quality program. The contractor's quality program should be requested in the solicitation and submitted as a part of the bid. Inadequate or nonexistent quality programs are indications of the contractor's potential for failure to meet buyer requirements. A well-documented quality program is only an indication that the contractor has an understanding of quality while prior demonstrated performance will confirm that the contractor has the capability of delivering quality.

I. Summary

There is a need for project personnel to ensure valid procedures are in place to guide the build of the product or service. The planning documentation provides that guide while leaving more time for the project manager to deal with unanticipated activities. Moreover, the anticipation of difficult areas allows more time to develop solutions and methods for avoiding areas with a high degree of risk. The anticipation of potential problem areas and the establishment of procedures will initiate the process, but the interest and emphasis of all project personnel is essential to ensure the end product is quality, i.e., meets the customer's requirements.

The cost of a project includes waste that results from weaknesses in a quality program or lack of an effective quality program. The assignment of quality costs in two categories, cost of quality and cost of non-quality, defines the additional costs which do not contribute to providing the product or service. Understanding the distribution of these costs facilitates a positive change to reduce non-quality costs.

Chapter IV   Cost of Quality

A. Cost of Quality

Cost of quality is the total price of all efforts to achieve product or service quality. This includes all work to build a product or service that conforms to the requirements as well as all work resulting from nonconformance to the requirements [155].

This definition provides a basis for measuring the cost of quality. It may be used to compare the cost of an end product to determine the difference from a similar product. In this way, a comparative measure can be used to assess the added cost for failing to meet quality requirements. Information on the Toyota automobile provides such an example [93, 209].

The efficiency of the Toyota Production System can be measured in dollars: The average Japanese automobile costs only two-thirds as much to make as the average American automobile, even though wages are near parity. After adding shipping costs and import duties, the Japanese automobile still costs $1,300 less than the American automobile.

The difference in price between the Toyota and an average American automobile is attributed to the quality orientation at Toyota for a net savings to produce a similar automobile. There is a cost of quality regardless of whether the expenditures are for work that conforms to the requirement or for rework of nonconforming products. The Toyota approach to building automobiles is a defect prevention system that consumes resources only for conforming work.

A pure quality system assures that expenditures to meet the customers' requirements are for actions that lead to a conforming product or service. Measuring the cost of quality, both in the sense of conforming and nonconforming work, must be accomplished to determine the total cost of the product or service and the opportunities presented by eliminating existing nonconforming activities. The quality system should have only expenditures for conforming activities to produce an end product.

Currently, many projects are not measuring the cost of nonconformance activities. The few that have measured the costs of quality reveal that several projects have extra costs in excess of 20 percent of the total cost of the project because of the lack of quality procedures. In many recent projects, 12 to 20 percent of the project costs can be attributed to waste. This does not include those projects which were never completed or those that had cost overruns in excess of 100 percent.

The typical project should have a goal of between 3 to 5 percent of the total value as the cost of a quality program, depending upon the type of project and its total dollar value. For example, a research and development project would have greater need for a larger quality program budget than would a project in a mature industry producing a product which replicates another project.

The general areas of cost for a quality system are listed in Figure IV.1. These categories of cost may represent an increase of cost in one area and a reduction

Cost of Conformance	Cost of Nonconformance
• Planning	• Scrap
• Training and indoctrination	• Rework
• Process control	• Expediting
• Field testing	• Additional material or inventory
• Product design validation	• Warranty repairs or service
• Process validation	• Complaint handling
• Test and evaluation	• Liability judgments
• Quality audits	• Product recalls
• Maintenance and calibration	• Product corrective actions
• Other	

Figure IV.1. Conformance versus Nonconformance Costs

of cost in another. For example, an improvement of process validation, a cost increase, may reduce scrap and rework, and thus, decrease total project cost.

Quality programs also have costs that are not apparent. The general categories of "additional direct costs" includes the areas below.

Cost to build right the first time. Planning and implementation of a quality program is costly and consumes many man-hours from managers and workers. The maintenance of a quality program is also a direct cost to the corporation. Time is used to indoctrinate individuals into the quality orientation and upgrade the facilities needed to accommodate a quality environment. The cost of establishing, maintaining and building on a quality program must be included in the price of products and services sold, and must be a part of the ongoing financial analyses.

Training programs. The individuals involved in building a product or delivering a service must have the knowledge, skills, and abilities to accomplish assigned tasks. These upgrades to the human resource capabilities can be achieved through corporate-sponsored training programs. Selecting and acquiring necessary training is accomplished through an analysis of the knowledge and skill requirements for each job. The knowledge and skill elements are defined for the training program.

Project training requirements should be assessed during the concept phase and all training accomplished during the planning phase. Skill and knowledge training, where possible, should be accomplished by the corporation prior to assignment of personnel to the project. Training at the project level should be reserved for team building, familiarization with the unique aspects of the project, and familiarization with the standards, procedures, and policies of the project.

Statistical Process Control (SPC) costs. Implementation of statistical process control procedures is an additional cost over a project without statistical means of monitoring and controlling the work. The cost of SPC varies with the sophistication and complexity of the work to be accomplished. Work of a nature that requires environmental control, high-grade materials, sterile environment, and precision cuttings will greatly benefit from SPC, although the cost of implementation will be high.

B. Cost of Non-Quality

The cost of a quality system is often viewed as a negative because errors in work have been traditionally accepted as a cost of doing business. Concepts such as "acceptable quality level," which sets an allowable defect rate, permit variances from the customers' requirements by ignoring a small number of defects from vendors and suppliers. Any system or process that will accept defective parts, materials, or services adds cost to the product or service.

The cost of non-quality is seldom identified in projects or companies because these extra costs reflect poorly on management. Managers do not want to publicize the costs, or negative profits, associated with accomplishing a task, job, or project. This situation, if allowed to continue, will have a significant impact on the profits as well as the competitive standing of a company.

There is insufficient data to make conclusive assessments of the cost of quality or the cost of non-quality for all types of projects. Indications are that the additional cost of non-quality is in the range of 12 to 20 percent as compared to a should-cost of 3 to 5 percent of sales. This general comparison of quality versus non-quality costs shows a difference of approximately 10 percent. In a competitive situation, this difference between a project with a quality program and the project without a quality program could make the difference between profit and loss.

Some of the major areas of cost for quality versus non-quality are discussed below. This discussion highlights the difference in where the money is spent to achieve the same desired output, although the result is either quality or non-quality output.

Waste of time and material. The waste of time and material is apparent when work has to be redone just to meet the minimum requirements. This waste of time and material represents manpower productivity losses through efforts to disassemble major assemblies or the scraping of components to start anew. Material costs include the cost of acquisition, storage, losses through damage, and any deterioration while in storage.

Rework of poor quality products. Reworking products is a distinct and separate type of work that requires special skills and knowledge to restore an item to the specified performance values. Special tools may be required to disassemble the product or special jigs to secure the component while rework is being accomplished. The rework is not a continuous flow type of work that is amenable to production techniques.

Additional material. The material actually used in rework of a product is not representative of the additional material required to be purchased. There can be no logical estimates for rework and the resultant material requirements. Thus there is a cost for the difference between the material used and the material required for doing the work right the first time.

Delays in schedule. Delays in schedule require additional money because the work process becomes less efficient with interrupted flows of work. Personnel are often waiting for the opportunity to start on work that is pending a rework situation. The deferred schedule on large projects can have a major impact when payment for work completed (i.e., earned value) is delayed until the project meets a milestone. The cost of money (i.e., interest) can easily erode the profit picture.

Product and service image. The public's image of a product or service will often be the determining factor for subsequent purchases. A poor product or service image can create loss of sales to former purchasers and potential purchasers seeking advise from former users. A quality product cannot guarantee a follow-on sale, but it will not preclude one.

Corporate image. The public's image of a corporation will often influence sales of the corporation's products and services. Quality products and service delivered to consumers will establish the corporation's standards. This will carry forward to ensure the image is favorable for new and existing product and service lines.

C. The Five Major Cost Categories of Quality

From a quality program perspective, the cost categories and their distribution must be understood to effectively change a situation to improve the quality of products and service. The understanding is easier when the categories of failure costs are codified and explained.

1. Prevention Cost

This is the cost to plan and execute a project so that it will be error-free. Some areas of prevention cost include planning of the scope, budget, performance and duration to meet customer requirements. This activity may be considered an investment for quality.

Training. Training required to upgrade skills and for orientation to the project must be matched with the complexity of the work, the level of expertise required, and the resident skills/knowledge of the project personnel.

Process capability studies. These need to be conducted to ensure all planned processes will meet the performance requirements of the product specifications. If the planned process is not capable of meeting the specifications, alternative processes will need to be considered.

Surveys of vendors/suppliers. These are conducted to determine the capability of vendors/suppliers to provide the proper grade of parts, components, materials, and services. These surveys are needed before initiation of the project and will encompass the quality control procedures used by the manufacturers and vendors as well as integration procedures. Vendor/supplier capabilities to provide quality inputs to the project's product is considered essential to the total process of meeting the customer's requirements.

Surveys of subcontractors. These determine the capabilities and quality orientation of the subcontractors' personnel and are essential to building a quality product. The project must include the subcontractors as part of the quality team in any planning and execution.

2. Appraisal Cost

This is the cost of evaluating the processes and the outputs of the processes to ensure the product is error-free. Maintenance of the processes through continual evaluation will provide the means to produce an error-free product. Evaluating the outputs (or products) will identify defects before delivery to the customer.

Inspection and testing of the products determines whether the product conforms to requirements and provides a means of identifying nonconforming products. This is a function under quality control, i.e., inspect and test to the quality plan and specifications.

Maintenance of inspection and test equipment ensures that resources used to measure the product are calibrated and in proper working order. These measurement instruments are the means to validate that the product meets the requirements as defined in the specifications.

Cost to process and report inspection data relates to the cost of human resources, equipment and time that is consumed in handling and reviewing the data. This is a requirement if the information is to have any affect on the quality of the product.

Design reviews are incremental steps that occur between the owner and the project to ensure the design meets the owner's requirements. Design reviews are sometimes labeled preliminary design review, critical design review, and final design review—a process of successive development of the design until the customer has full visibility into the final design of the product.

Internal design review and walk-throughs are peer reviews by which designs and design implementations are evaluated through the use of internal resources or cooperative support groups. Internal evaluations of products and processes are often used for complex projects prior to formal reviews with the customer. They may be used to confirm or validate processes by experts from other corporate projects.

Expense reviews are comparative reviews of the budget against the actual cost of performing work. The purpose is to determine the variance between the two and provide corrective action for future work.

3. Internal Failure Cost

Internal failure cost is a cost incurred to correct an identified defect before the customer receives the product. This does not include the appraisal costs to identify defects.

Scrap and rework result in wasted material and time. The costs to correct the defects are included in this category. Any cost associated with the involvement of external expertise or processes is also included.

Charges related to late payment of bills include the failure to pay invoices within the time specified or within the time when discounts are given.

Inventory costs that are a direct result of defects include extra inventory requirements for materials and parts to correct defects and the associated cost of money to maintain the added inventory.

Engineering change costs related to correcting a design error are sometimes required when the original design was flawed, not meeting the customer's requirements. Correcting such errors can have significant cost impacts. This does not include design changes resulting from a customer's change of scope.

Infant mortality is related to premature failure of products. Premature failures may be identified during a product's stress testing or early in its life cycle. Costs would encompass new designs, new materials or components, and other corrective actions to meet the customer's functional requirements.

Correcting documentation relates to the changing of documentation because the original was in error or incomplete. Any change to the documentation because of failure to anticipate the information or because of incorrect typing is considered an additional cost.

4. External Failure Cost

This cost category relates to all errors not detected and corrected before delivery to the customer. The external failure cost would include some of the areas identified under internal failure cost, such as scrap and rework and inventory costs, but would be after the customer took possession of the product.

Warranty cost is the cost of repair or replacement of the product to meet the functionality and merchantability specified or implied in the warranty.

Field service personnel training cost are incurred to train personnel to perform repair or replacement services at the customer's location or in a service shop. This is specialized training to identify the defect and effect repairs/replacement to restore the product to the level of functionality stated or implied in the contract.

Recall costs result from notifying customers of a fault in the product and the locations for obtaining repairs or replacements as well as the cost of the repairs and replacements.

Product liability suits lead to costs of legal representation and any resultant judgments against the corporation for products that fail to meet the stated or implied functionality or safety requirements.

Complaint handling requires the maintenance of a system to handle complaints and potential repair or replacement costs as well as returned products.

Future business losses result because poor quality leads to fewer sales and fewer sales result in lower project profits. They can also result in increased project costs through reduced economies of scale. Economy of scale results when the business base is sufficiently large to permit purchases of material or use of human resources in more efficient groups and the use of more efficient methods and equipment.

5. Measurement and Test Equipment

This is the capital cost of equipment used to perform prevention and appraisal activities. The equipment to perform the prevention activities would normally include the measurement of processes that must be maintained within specified bounds to produce a product. An example of this could be the continuous measurement of the chemical composition for developing film to assure the chemicals are of the proper mixture, time and temperature for a type of film. The equipment to perform the appraisal activities includes all measurement devices used to check the size, shape, hardness, volume, etc., of a product. An example is a micrometer caliper that is used to measure the diameter of a shaft.

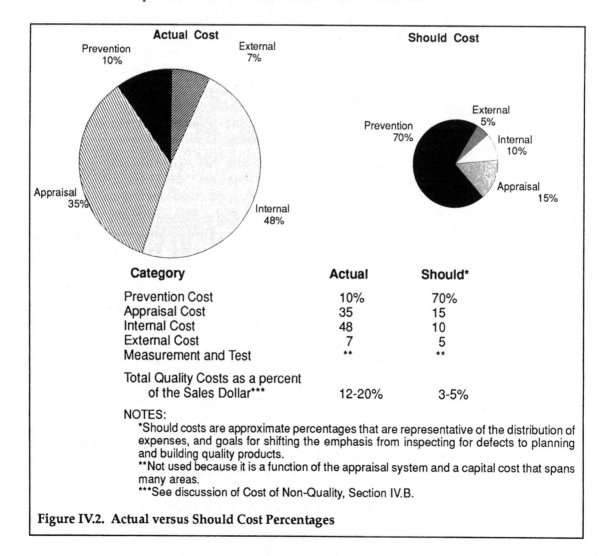

Category	Actual	Should*
Prevention Cost	10%	70%
Appraisal Cost	35	15
Internal Cost	48	10
External Cost	7	5
Measurement and Test	**	**
Total Quality Costs as a percent of the Sales Dollar***	12-20%	3-5%

NOTES:
*Should costs are approximate percentages that are representative of the distribution of expenses, and goals for shifting the emphasis from inspecting for defects to planning and building quality products.
**Not used because it is a function of the appraisal system and a capital cost that spans many areas.
***See discussion of Cost of Non-Quality, Section IV.B.

Figure IV.2. Actual versus Should Cost Percentages

Actual versus Should Cost

The division of costs between the five categories discussed in this section can be categorized into actual and should cost percentage [49, 46]. Figure IV.2 is representative of the relative scale between the actual and should cost categories. Note that both actual and should cost columns total to 100 percent. Total dollar value of the should column will always be less than the actual column for successful quality programs.

Comparison of actual and should cost percentages shows a heavier emphasis on prevention cost and less on appraisal. It is the modern approach to quality to shift the investment to doing the job correctly the first time and reducing wastes associated with rework, customer dissatisfaction, and loss of reputation.

D. The Opportunities Available

General categories where cost can be saved reflect opportunities to change procedures currently in existence and achieve new economies. The listed categories are only samples of areas that may be addressed to reduce burdens on the project.

Just-In-Time

Just-In-Time (JIT) is the concept of zero inventory. It is a concept and practice that eradicates the idea of inventory in a manufacturing plant and can be applied to projects to gain similar efficiencies. Parts are not kept in warehouses, waiting to be moved to a production line. The concept was started when the realization came that parts in inventory are a waste of time, money, and people resulting from the added cost of storage at a distant location from the production line, the movement of parts to the production line, the loss of parts through damage from handling, and the cost of the inventory before it is needed [93, 210-211].

JIT forces the system to produce only parts that meet requirements because there is no stockpile from which to obtain qualified parts if the existing ones do not meet the requirements. The practice forces individuals to pay attention to the quality of materials, workmanship, and finished products.

In a project environment, it is most desirable for the materials and components to arrive at the precise time of need rather than several days or weeks ahead of the need date. Early arrival of large bulk materials often causes problems with storage space as well as the potential for deterioration through weather or loss through pilferage. Climate-sensitive equipment requires controlled environment storage. All these items add cost to a project and increase the risk of having to purchase more materials; more than are actually required than if the materials were delivered at the precise time of need.

An exception to JIT is where social or economic benefits are greater external to the project than internal to the project. In China the manufacture of bricks is a major industry operated in such a way as to maintain the work force at an even level. Bricks are moved to the construction site as many as three years in advance and stacked in neat order. The police conduct periodic inspections to determine whether the stacks are missing any bricks (i.e., any irregular stacks). For a public bath facility in Beijing, the bricks were in place more than one year before the start of construction.

JIT affects quality of the product by requiring changes in the number of defects in parts in the system feeding the manufacturing process. The number of defects and the seriousness of the defects must be reduced to a level that will not impact the manufacturing process. The quality of the process (process

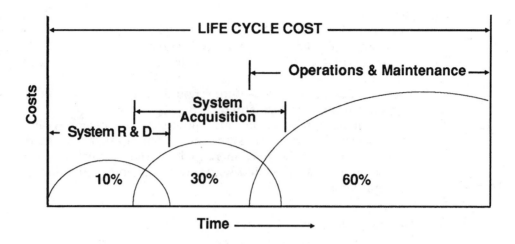

Figure IV.3. Life Cycle Cost Model

control) requires adjustment to tighten the variances in processing. A reduction in variances in processing would tend to reduce variances in the product being manufactured [48, 317].

Product Life Cycle Cost

The cost of a product—that is the development, fabrication, operation and maintenance, and disposal of a single unit of product— is referred to as the life cycle cost. The traditional model of product life cycle cost has three parts: Research and Development Cost, Acquisition Cost, and Operation and Maintenance Cost. These three parts are estimated to consume 10 percent, 30 percent, and 60 percent, respectively, of the total cost. Figure IV.3 depicts this life cycle cost [178, 17-2].

This model reflects traditional thinking for the division of product costs because the research and development, manufacture, and operating functions have been separate and distinct areas of responsibility. Linking the three areas of cost and considering each one's cost implications for the other gives a situation which can change the total cost of product ownership. For example, the traditional $100 million project would have $10 million invested in research and development costs, $30 million in acquisition (building, construction, fabrication, implementation) costs, and $60 million in operation and maintenance costs. Changing this traditional model, a 10 percent increase in research and development investment might increase the project acquisition cost by 1 percent while decreasing the operation and maintenance cost by 12 percent. This example of change is reflected in the following table.

This simple model illustrates the need to investigate all areas of cost to obtain the cost of ownership, or life cycle cost, to determine the best approach to designing, building, and operating/maintaining a project's product.

	Traditional	Change Model
Research and Development	10,000,000	11,000,000
Acquisition	30,000,000	30,300,000
Operations and Maintenance	60,000,000	52,800,000
Total	100,000,000	94,100,000
Savings		5,900,000

Another aspect of the life cycle cost is not suggested by Figure IV.3 is the increasing cost of usage as a function of the products life. As the age of the unit increases, measured in years, operating hours, or operating cycles, the maintenance costs increase due to failure or degradation of performance of components. An example of this phenomena is a new automobile which may require some initial adjustments over the first 2,000 miles and occasional maintenance such as tune-ups, replacement of a battery, replacement of tires, and changing wiper blades. As the automobile passes the 60,000 mile mark, however, there may be some major repairs indicated such as a transmission overhaul, replacement of the water pump, alternator, power steering pump, and air conditioner compressor, or a major overhaul of the engine. The cost of the normal replacement of battery, tires, and hoses is relatively low as compared to the overhaul of a transmission or engine, thus, these costs tend to increase over time.

In addition to these maintenance costs, the product eventually incurs a competitive disadvantage due to obsolescence.

Product Maturity

New products, whether one of a kind or multiple units, have a maturity process for reliability over their life time. The newly introduced product tends to have relatively frequent failures as compared to products produced later on the experience curve. At the introduction of the product into service and operation, reliability tends to be low (or stated another way, repairs are frequently required). The number of repairs rapidly diminishes to a fairly even level over the product's normal design life and then rapidly increases as the product nears the end of its useful life.

This can be demonstrated using the bathtub curve which describes the distribution of the probability of failures of a large number of the same product over their useful life. The bathtub curve, shown in Figure IV.4, is composed of three distinct periods: infant mortality, normal operating, and wear-out. Failures during the infant mortality period are characterized by design or manufacturing flaws which become evident very quickly after the unit is placed in service. To prevent these from becoming external failures, the unit is placed in simulated normal usage in an attempt to pass through the infant mortality period. For electronic products this is called a burn-in while for computer software it is called alpha and beta tests. The probability of failures during the normal operating period is very low for most commercial products. During the wear-out period the probability of failure increases to the mean-time-to-failure and then starts decreasing as fewer and fewer units actually exceed design life

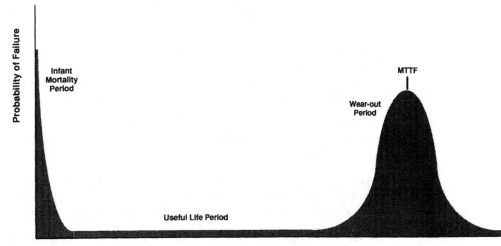

Figure IV.4. Bathtub Curve

by greater amounts. This assumes that the product is non-reparable or that no repairs are made. The useful life of a reparable product can be prolonged by replacement of parts as or before they fail.

Consider an industrial lighting lamp. If it is manufactured incorrectly, it is likely to failue quickly after being placed in service. If it is placed in operation in a burn in process that failure is likely to occur before the customer incurs the cost of installing it. The probability of failure once installed is quite low. As the unit approaches its design life, the probability of failure may resemble a normal curve.

Now returning to product maturity, consider how the bathtub curve might change from early production units to later units. As historical data is collected, causes of infant mortality failures are identified and corrected. As a result, the slope of this part of the curve becomes steeper and the product will emerge from the infant mortality period much more quickly. Thus, the testing or burn-in period can be reduced and the number of failures will decrease. This results in less cost to the producer and lower prices to the user. Empirical data from the normal operating period can also be used to identify causes of failures and lead to design or production changes which reduce the probability of failure even further in this period. This reduces the cost of operating the product. Similarly, identification of causes of failure in wear-out can result in modifications which actually extend the useful life of the product. All of these result in lower costs of using the product for the customer or client.

These phenomena are relevant in projects which produce only one unit as they typically involve the combination of products into the product of the project. If the products so combined are standard technology, i.e., relatively mature products, they should combine with a high degree of reliability and require relatively little debugging, as in software, or adjustments to achieve system validation and acceptance. On the otherhand, a project involving state-of-the-art products or technology will likely require extensive testing and debugging to achieve stable operation. In such cases, the cost will be greater.

Areas of Waste in Projects

Nine categories of waste have been identified that will assist project planners in anticipating the additional costs associated with nonconformance to requirements [58, 250].

Waste in rejects of completed work. Completed work does not conform to requirements (specifications) and is, therefore, an extra cost to the project.

Waste in design flaws. The design does not conform to requirements and is not a valid tool for building the project. Correction of the design and any work associated with faulty design is an extra cost to the project.

Waste in work-in-process. Flow of work is affected when work that is in process has to be stopped because of inadequate process capability, material is an improper grade, procedures are incorrect, or people are not trained. This stoppage of the smooth flow of work is an extra cost to the project.

Waste in motion for manpower. People who do not know, are not instructed, or are improperly instructed will waste motion in the project. This is an extra cost to the project.

Waste in management. Management personnel who improperly direct the work or direct work that is not required can consume human and material resources that do not contribute to the project. This is an extra cost to the project.

Waste in manpower. When personnel are placed on the wrong work, used for jobs in which they are not trained, are scheduled for the wrong phase of the project, or are made to wait for work because of improper scheduling, there is a loss of work effort that cannot be recovered. This is an extra cost to the project.

Waste in facilities. Facility waste can happen in many forms, but most notably as a result of improper usage or unnecessary activity. An example of improper facility use is ordering excess materials for storage on site in limited building space. Another is use of storage space to park vehicles when the space is needed for weather-sensitive materials. When material must then be stored in rented facilities it can result in an extra cost to the project.

Waste in expenses. Expenses that do not contribute to the completion of the project are waste. An example of this is the rental of a meeting room in a hotel when an office or large lobby would serve the purpose. Travel costs also fall into this category when individuals rent automobiles larger than required or stay on travel longer than necessary.

E. Summary

The cost of quality is a combination of factors that contribute to the preparation and delivery of a product to a customer. Cost of non-quality, however, is all expenditures that waste time, motion, material or other valuable resources. This non-quality cost is a point of contention in that the wastes are often assumed to be a given part of the process while in the modern context of quality there is no allowance for waste or defects. Acceptance of the extra burden of non-quality costs as a "cost of doing business" can materially affect the profit of a project.

The cost of quality is an investment in the future where the project manager anticipates the actions and resources required to successfully meet customer satisfaction. These actions include planning a project to the level of detail necessary for efficient implementation and operation, training the project team with the proper skills and indoctrination to perform the work, establishing a process whereby all engineering design is performed well in advance, and ensuring that materials going into the process are of the proper grade.

The trend is to place a prevention orientation in the process and reduce the inspection requirements. Inspections only reveal defects and have no part in the correction, or making the system whole. Costs associated with producing a quality product are much less than those associated with producing a non-quality product that must be repaired.

The use of statistical methods and quality tools facilitates early identification and resolution of problems that affect project effectiveness. The methods and tools, derived from the manufacturing area, are valid and pertinent to the project's work. Using proven processes in a proactive manner will increase the probability of success for the project.

Chapter V   Statistical Concepts and Quality Tools

A. Introduction

Many projects, because of their short-term and unique product character, do not directly use statistical concepts in the implementation phase. Products and services, however, from vendors, suppliers, and subcontractors are a part of the quality inherent in the project. These second tier participants can affect the outcome of the end product through actions that contribute to or detract from the quality aspects desired by the customer.

Project managers need knowledge of the statistical concepts, practices, and procedures used in building assemblies, components, and parts to ensure that second tier project providers are meeting the requirements of the customer. Although project managers may not have detailed knowledge of the statistical concepts, they should have a general understanding of the practices and procedures used to meet project standards.

The tools of modern quality management and their applications are important to any program of continuous quality improvement. Project managers knowledgeable of the tools can more effectively conduct continuous improvement programs to ensure that quality aspects of a project are in a constant state of improvement. Familiarity with these tools will assist the project manager in highlighting information, providing a structure for assessing information, and showing relationships among data for analysis.

B. Statistical Quality Control

Statistical quality control is the method used to measure variability in a product for evaluation and corrective actions. When the product exceeds the bounds of acceptability, based on statistical inference, the product can be rejected with reasonable assurance that it does not meet requirements. On the other hand, a product can be accepted with the same assurance, or level of confidence, that it does meet the standard.

Normal Distribution Curve

The most common statistical approach to measuring variability is with the normal distribution curve. Figure V.1 depicts a normal distribution curve with three standard deviations on each side of the mean.

As depicted, the normal distribution curve shows the concept of standard deviations and the area under the curve. The six standard deviations (plus three and minus three) encompass 99.73 percent of the area under the curve, while plus and minus one standard deviation includes 68.26 percent. The area beyond the three sigma points is the complement of the area under the six standard deviations, or 100 minus 99.73 to equal 0.27 percent.

For an actual normal curve developed through sampling and computing ranges of variation, the shape could be significantly different. A normal curve computed through data that has a wide variation between data points would be shallow and wide, while a normal curve computed from data with little variation would be tall and narrow. As stated, the variation in the data points determines the width of the standard deviations.

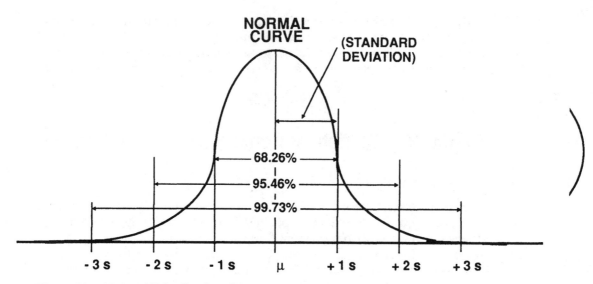

Figure V.1. Normal Distribution Curve

C. Quality Control Systems

Two major systems are used in statistical quality control: process control charts and acceptance sampling. These control charts are statistical techniques used for monitoring and evaluating variations in a process. Acceptance sampling is acceptance or rejection of an already produced lot. The reason for using quality control checks is to measure the degree to which the product or service is conforming to standards and whether there are unfavorable trends in the data. Standards can be specified internally, within the organization, or they can be imposed by the customer.

Standards for products and services are critical to the process of satisfying customer requirements. Before the conformance of a product can be measured, standards that describe specific requirements for the product must be developed. Quality control techniques can be applied to determine product conformance to the standards.

Standards for products are defined in quantitative measures with a range of acceptable variation. The range of variation may be customer-driven or process-driven. The customer's requirements may be well within the capability of the process and available technology to permit conformance to the requirement. On the other hand, the requirement may be beyond the capability of the existing process and a new process may be required. In either case, the standard, or requirement, is not changed to accept lesser grades than the requirement.

The two quality control techniques for determining whether the products meet standards and for receipt of materials or parts for the project are described below. These two techniques are the heart of the manufacturing process [62].

Process Control Charts

Process control charts identify the allowable range of variation for a particular product characteristic. By specifying upper and lower bounds of allowable variation, a control chart is created which can be used as a tool to evaluate product conformance. The upper boundary on the chart is identified as the UCL or the Upper Control Limit. Similarly, the lower boundary on the chart is the LCL or the Lower Control Limit. Between these upper and lower limits is the process average. The process average is the mean of the averages for the samples taken over a long period of time. The upper and lower limits may represent weight, temperature, shoe size and other characteristics of a product.

A control chart is represented by the normal curve turned on its side. The upper control limit (top) is the right hand side of the normal curve while the lower control limit (bottom) is the left hand side of the normal curve. The process average is the average of the sample averages and it is exactly half-way between the upper and lower limits. Figure V.2 shows the normal curve percentages as an overlay to the control chart.

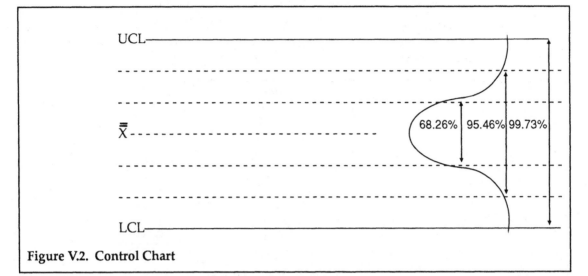

Figure V.2. Control Chart

Plotting data, either individual or averages of small samples, on the control chart will show the variation from the mean (average) of the product characteristic specification. These plots depict the measured data and indicate the degree of conformance to the requirement. Figure V.3 shows a control chart depicting a system "in control" because all data points are within the control limits (plus or minus three standard deviations).

In Figure V.3, a control chart is used to track the variation in product characteristic over time. This control chart has twenty-three points representing the twenty-three sample averages. This process is "in control" because points fall between the UCL and LCL. A careful examination of the chart shows no trend where the data points are moving toward the upper or lower limits.

Developing a control chart is relatively easy. The product specification determines the mid-point of the control chart and the variation is three standard deviations, representing the range of acceptable variation from the specified value. There are two methods of setting the UCL and LCL.

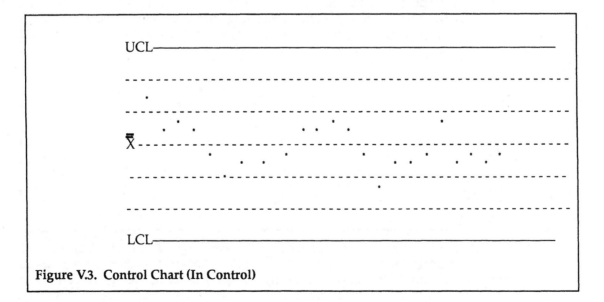

Figure V.3. Control Chart (In Control)

The product is not being produced. To find the upper and lower limits of the control chart, management identifies the point of variation at which the characteristic of the product is unacceptable. This sets the initial allowable variation in the product. The allowable variation limit is three sigma points on the control chart and represents the initial UCL and LCL.

The product is being produced. Samples are taken of the product and measurements made. The measurements provide the data from which standard deviations are calculated. The following example shows the calculations.

Item Number	Weight, lb. (x)	$(x - \mu)^2$
1	4.9	0.02778
2	5.0	0.00444
3	5.1	0.00111
4	5.2	0.01778
5	5.3	0.05444
6	5.5	0.18778
7	4.7	0.13444
8	4.8	0.07111
9	5.1	0.00111
Total	45.6	0.50000

Key:
x = Sample weight
μ = Average (Mean) of the sample weights
s = Standard deviation of Sample

Calculated Values:

Mean	5.0666 (rounded to 5.07)
Variance	0.0625
Standard deviation	0.25

The mean (μ) equals the sum of the weights (45.6 pounds) divided by the number of samples (nine) for a result of 5.07 pounds. The variance, a measure of the amount of dispersion from the mean, is the sum of the squared differences between the mean and each sample value, divided by the number of samples (nine) minus one, or eight. The square root of the variance (0.0625 pound) is the standard deviation (0.25 pound).

This example gives a standard deviation equal to 0.25 pound. The upper control limit value is equal to three standard deviations, or 0.75 pound plus the average of 5.07 pounds, i.e., 5.82 pounds. The lower control limit is the mean minus three standard deviations, or 4.32. For illustrative purposes the values have been calculated below.

UCL	3 s	5.816666
	2 s	5.566666
	1 s	5.316666
	μ	5.066666
	-1 s	4.816666
	-2 s	4.566666
LCL	-3 s	4.316666

In the example of the computation of the control chart, no data points exceeded the upper or lower limits. Thus, the clustering of data points does not indicate an out of control situation. The illustration, however, should not be accepted as a complete solution because the weight variations (plus 0.75 and minus 0.75 pound) may exceed the product tolerance limits. If that is the case, the upper and lower control limits would be unacceptable for this product characteristic. If the process capability is truly represented by the above data, an alternative process with less variability may be required.

Identification of an adverse pattern should cause an evaluation of the process. Sometimes, mechanical devises will have parts work loose or wear. If an adverse pattern develops, independently check each element of the process while holding other elements stable to help identify the problem.

Control charts provide an easy, systematic way of identifying whether a product or service is within specified boundaries. Control charts are versatile tools because they can be developed for many products and services. The key to successful quality control using control charts is to establish the charts and routinely analyze the data points to identify overall product quality or variations in that quality.

There are several variations of control charts and the patterns associated with them. There are five categories of control charts that have patterns which one should be able to recognize. Examples are shown in Figures V.4a-e.

In Figure V.4a, the circled data point illustrates a sample average that is out of control, i.e., it exceeds the lower control limit. This chart with nine sample averages indicates an abnormality that requires investigation to determine the cause of the variation.

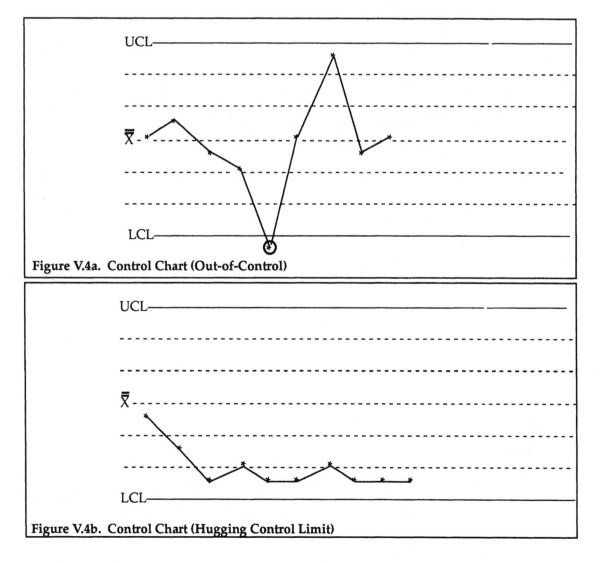

Figure V.4a. Control Chart (Out-of-Control)

Figure V.4b. Control Chart (Hugging Control Limit)

Figure V.4b depicts seven of nine sample averages "hugging" the lower control limit to indicate the process average has moved to the lower values. This change is an abnormality that requires correction because even a slight change would move the data points outside of the lower control limit. As a rule of thumb, it is considered abnormal if two of three, three of seven, or four of ten data points fall within the outer one-third of the chart.

Figure V.4c depicts thirteen sample averages that form a repeating pattern of data points over a range of the control chart. This change occurs in response to regular changes in the process average. This variation shows an abnormal pattern of change which must be investigated.

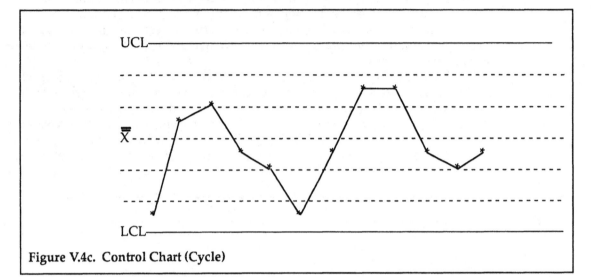

Figure V.4c. Control Chart (Cycle)

Figure V.4d shows two plots of sample averages, one increasing and one decreasing. This abnormal trend is formed when seven or more consecutive data points reflect a steadily increasing or decreasing pattern or a progressive pattern over time.

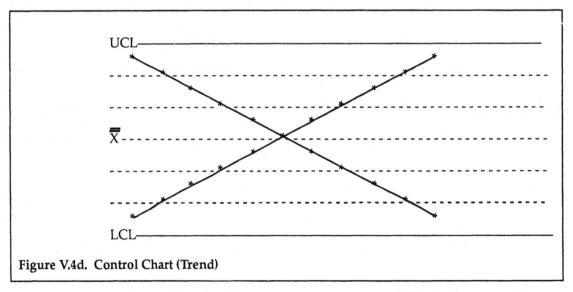

Figure V.4d. Control Chart (Trend)

Figure V.4e shows two plots of sample averages that have consecutive data points on one side of the midpoint (average). As a rule of thumb, it is considered abnormal if seven consecutive points, ten of eleven, or twelve of fourteen data points are above or below the process average. This measurable change may be tightly grouped or more random.

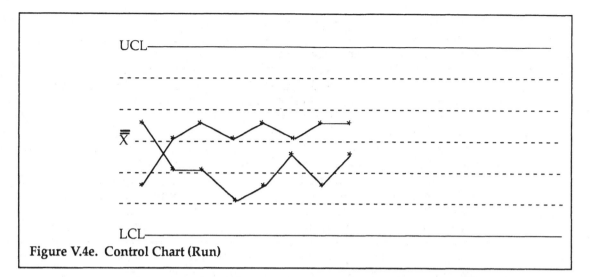

Figure V.4e. Control Chart (Run)

The control charts reflect representative examples of the types of patterns that could be encountered in any process of sampling and plotting data. The control charts provide only the results of the sampling and do not include measures for adjusting the process to meet the requirements or give indications as to the reason for the patterns. The process must be evaluated to determine the reasons for deviation from the prescribed standard.

D. Acceptance Sampling

The purpose of acceptance sampling is to determine whether or not the lot conforms to the specifications or standards necessary to support the overall project requirements. Inspection and test standards must be established to ensure that procedures are adequate to determine whether a lot is conforming or nonconforming to specifications. Inspection and test standards could include external visual inspection, stressing of materials, disassembly and visual inspection, destruction of the item, artificial environmental stressing, or temperature cycling. The type of inspection or test procedure must be defined for any acceptance sampling [62][166].

In addition to the standards for inspection and testing, standards must be set for qualification of the sampled lot. These standards focus on the parametric values to be achieved during any inspection or test. Standards, for example, could be set to include such qualifications as no visual defects, no defects in the materials, and no deviations in the size of the item. This would be consistent with the "zero defect" philosophy. Or, if this is not achievable, standards can be derived from conventional acceptance sampling plan tables such as in *Military Handbook 53-1A* [166].

The way to ensure conformance of each product is to inspect and test each item. Unfortunately, 100 percent inspection is time consuming and expensive and still may not guarantee zero defects. Random sampling may be used to check the characteristics and attributes of a given lot of goods. Based on the results of the random sample, the lot of goods can either be accepted or rejected.

There are several factors that must be determined prior to performing acceptance sampling. It is important to select a sample size that will provide sufficient information about the larger lot of goods without costing a great deal of money. In addition to selecting a sample size, it is necessary to determine the maximum number of defects in the sample that will cause rejection of the lot. The combination of sample size and number of defects in that sample provides an estimate of the overall conformance of the lot.

Sample size is directly related to how well the sample represents the characteristic of the lot. Small samples are not normally representative of large lots. However, large samples are expensive to assess and may not provide noticeably better estimates. Therefore, it is important to identify the sample size that will serve as a good representative of the larger lot.

Another important variable in acceptance sampling is the number of defects before a lot is rejected. The number of defects is determined by management. For example, the number of acceptable defects may vary from as many as 20 in 100 to as few as 3 in a 1,000. The 20 in 100 represents one in five, or 20 percent defects, while the 3 in 1,000 represents 0.3 percent of the sample defective. Establishing the limit on the number of defects which will cause the entire lot to be rejected is a responsibility of management.

Figure V.5 graphically portrays an acceptance sampling plan for a lot of 100 units. The allowable number of defects is 2 and the sample size is 15. This sample of 15 units will provide information about the overall quality of the lot of 100 units. Each of the 15 units in the sample are tested. The maximum number of defects was set at 2. This means that the sample of 15 units will be tested and if 2 or less defects are found in the sample, the lot of 100 units will be accepted. However, if 3 or more defects are found in the sample, the entire lot of 100 units will be rejected.

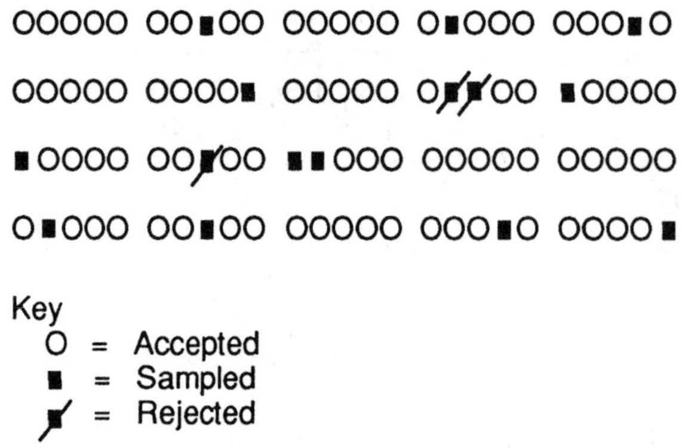

Figure V.5 . Acceptance Sample

The outcome of this acceptance sampling plan results in rejection of the entire lot of 100 units because 3 bad parts were found in the sample. If only 2 defects were found in the sample, the lot of 100 units would have been accepted as being within the acceptance standards for this project.

E. Example of a Quality Control System

The most important concept is that quality control is a vital element of any organization. Product characteristics and attributes vary between individual items because of variations in the process for building the items. Quality control does not always require rigid statistical techniques and formulas. It can be adapted to any business, provided there is impetus for maintaining a certain level of quality [156].

Quality assurance is the backbone of Office Electronics, Inc. (OEI) because they realize the value of providing high-quality products to their customers. OEI established six major areas in which they concentrate on quality throughout the manufacturing process. Figure V.6 summarizes the quality assurance program developed and maintained by OEI.

Incoming material inspection. Quality starts with the materials that make up the final product. Therefore, it is essential to be certain the materials used for the product are of the correct grade. Random samples of two sheets, 1-foot square, are cut from a sample of no less than 10 percent of the total quantity

QUALITY ASSURANCE PROGRAM
OFFICE ELECTRONICS, INC.

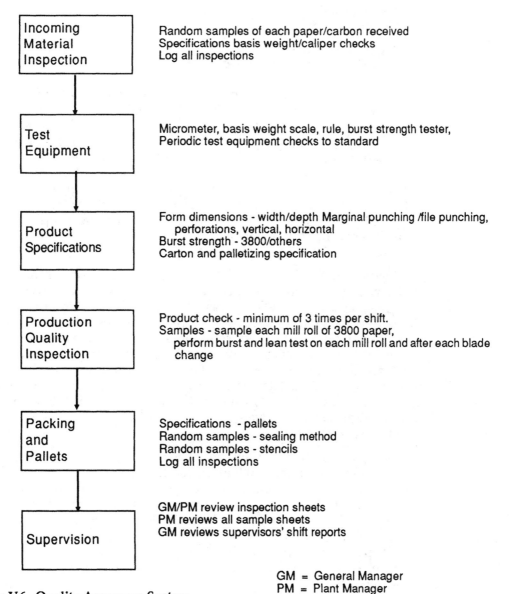

Figure V.6. Quality Assurance System

received. These sample sheets are subject to tests of thickness, weight and appearance. Each type of paper must meet predetermined specifications. Standards have been set and some variation is allowed; however, there are defined upper and lower bounds that must not be exceeded. All inspections of incoming materials are to be logged and then reviewed by the plant manager.

Test equipment. Each plant is required to maintain and use specific pieces of equipment. It is essential to use equipment that has been maintained and checked to accurately record quality control information. The supervisor checks and records the performance of all the machines at the start of a shift and four times during the shift. Listed below is the test equipment required at each operation and the function it performs in the quality control process.

One micrometer caliper. Used to measure the thickness of paper or carbon samples.

One basis weight scale. Used to measure the weight of paper samples. This machine is tested quarterly.

One 20-inch steel rule. Used to measure the dimensions of samples (length, width and center-to-center spacing).

One burst strength tester. Used for measuring the burst strength of perforations. This machine is calibrated quarterly for accuracy.

Product specifications. This phase of quality control checks the form dimensions and burst strengths of the products. Standards are specified for width, depth, marginal punching (size and location of the holes), perforations and every other product characteristic that could be tested or verified. Each standard is defined in detail as to how the product should look when it is finished and any allowable variation is clearly identified. For example, the paper is punched with holes on the left and right aligning margins. Each marginal hole should be 5/36 inch plus or minus 1/64 inch in diameter. Deviations from the standard are not allowed. The paper's burst strength is standardized to make certain the product is not subject to unintentional ripping. Standards are specified for the burst strength of the different types of paper.

Production quality inspection. Once the product is manufactured, and it conforms to all previous quality checks, it must pass one more phase of quality control—product check. During this phase of quality verification, samples of the product are taken and subjected to various tests. These product tests include burst tests and lean tests. Burst tests examine the product's ability to stand up to pressure. Standards are specified for the paper's minimum and maximum burst strength. Lean tests examine the product's ability to stand up straight when stacked. It is unacceptable for a 1-foot stack of paper to lean more than 1/4 inch in any direction. Any nonconformance to standards is a red flag and must be corrected immediately. Product checks are routinely administered at least three times per shift.

Packaging and pallets. Quality control does not stop with a quality product at OEI; the product must arrive at the customer's office in excellent condition. There are specific standards required for packaging and shipping of the final paper product. Samples of the packaging are routinely taken to ensure the quality of the product throughout the entire manufacturing process. Specifications are identified for pallets. Cartons of paper may be stacked no more than five cartons high. Cartons must be placed on the pallet in accordance with regulations, based on the size of the paper. There are even standards that specify the size, 3/8 inch, and positioning of the stenciling for each carton.

Supervision. A supervisor's job is to ensure people are performing their jobs in accordance with the standards set by the organization. The supervisor performs quality control at many levels. It is the supervisor's job to check every machine at the start of each shift; check and record the performance of all the machines four times per shift; review samples of the product during different phases of product development; perform burst and lean tests; and spot-check finished cartons on a regular basis.

OEI provides quality confidence to its customers. Because they take a great deal of time and interest in manufacturing and delivering quality products, it is apparent that they perceive quality as the backbone to success. The comprehensive, structured system for maintaining quality control within this environment has proven successful.

F. Check List for Developing a Quality Control System

Plans can and should be tailored to a specific product or item. Listed below are some points to consider when developing a quality control system[156].

- Examine the product or item.
- Identify the desired level of performance.
- Set standards to support that level of performance.
- Examine the various techniques available to establish a quality control system.
- Decide which quality control system is suitable for your needs.
- Establish the criteria for maintaining the quality control system (number of defects, sample size, rejection/acceptance criteria).
- Develop the quality control system based on the above six criteria.
- Maintain and examine the quality control system.
- Evaluate the effectiveness of the quality control system.
- Make necessary adjustments to the quality control system.
- Periodically re-evaluate the quality control system to make sure it is still providing information about the performance of the product.

G. The Tools of Modern Quality Management

The tools of modern quality management relate to problem solving through uniform processes that provide information which leads to recognizing process changes and correcting them. The problem-solving tools most commonly used are listed below [58].

Pareto diagrams. These diagrams rank defects in order of frequency of occurrence, using a histogram, to depict 100 percent of the defects. Defects with the most frequent occurrence are prime areas of opportunity to improve the situation, and should be first in order of corrective actions.

The two Pareto diagrams in Figure V.7 illustrate the value of ranking defects. Before improvement, the number of defects for "improper rotation" is approximately 42, which represents 40 percent of the total number of defects. This defect rate is more than three times the next item, "noise." Following the improvement actions by a corrective team, "improper rotation" is reduced to approximately 10 defects, or second in the order of defects.

Note that frequency of occurrence may not be the best criteria for ranking defects. It could cause corrective action to be directed to a frequently occurring defect which may have trivial consequences. Rather, the Pareto analysis should generally be applied on a measure of the relative importance, e.g., costs, failure consequences, or impact on customer.

Cause and effect diagrams. These diagrams provide a structured means to analyze the inputs to a process for identification of the causes of errors. The cause and effect diagram, also called fishbone diagram because of its resemblance to the skeleton of a fish, consists of eight major inputs to a quality process to permit the characterization of each input. Some diagrams with fewer categories have been used in some situations to characterize a process, but the diagram with eight major categories is considered to be more encompassing for quality management purposes. Figure V.8 illustrates the cause and effect diagram

This diagram outlines the methodology used to identify major defects in a process. The eight input blocks represent the combination of resources or areas that will affect the process.

- Time is the calendar time required to perform a task of the process. All work requires time as a condition of performing a task whether it is accomplished by a human, a machine, or a chemical subprocess.
- Energy is the type and amount of power required for the project. Types of power could be electrical, diesel, or gasoline.

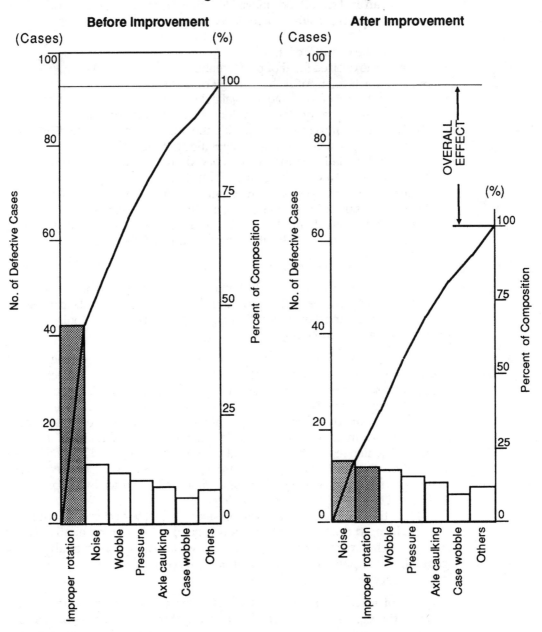

Figure V.7. Pareto Diagrams

- Machine is any type of machinery required on the project. This could be a lathe, truck, press, or workbench.
- Measurement is the system for measuring the process, product, and components of the process as well as the calibration devices for the measuring tools.
- Method is the system of policies and procedures for building the product. It includes subprocesses of the project such as prescribed standards for mixing cement, the use of special tools, or reporting data.
- Personnel are the human resources, both on and off the project, that have an input to the project requirements. The customer, senior management, workers, and project manager are included in this category.
- Material is all raw or processed material, parts, components, assemblies, or products used in building the product.

CAUSE AND EFFECT DIAGRAM

CAUSE AND EFFECT ANALYSIS

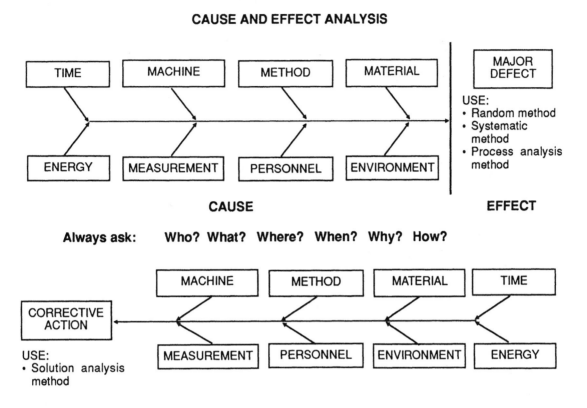

Figure V.8. Cause and Effect Diagram

- Environment is the natural or man-made conditions under which the project's product must be built and operate. This could include operation in a tropical jungle, a desert sandstorm, at a minus 30-degree Fahrenheit temperature, or a temperature range of minus 10 to plus 120 degrees Fahrenheit.

Histograms. These diagrams are vertical bars in a chart to show frequency of occurrence of items within a range of activity. For example, it may be useful to show the frequency of occurrence for the measured diameter of a machined cylinder to determine whether the process is normally distributed around the

Figure V.9. Histogram (Sample)

desired measurement or whether the sizes have a tendency to be skewed toward one side of the control limits. Histograms are useful to graphically depict data that may indicate a potential problem is about to occur.

Scatter diagrams. These diagrams are used to determine the relationship between two of more pieces of corresponding data. The data are plotted on an

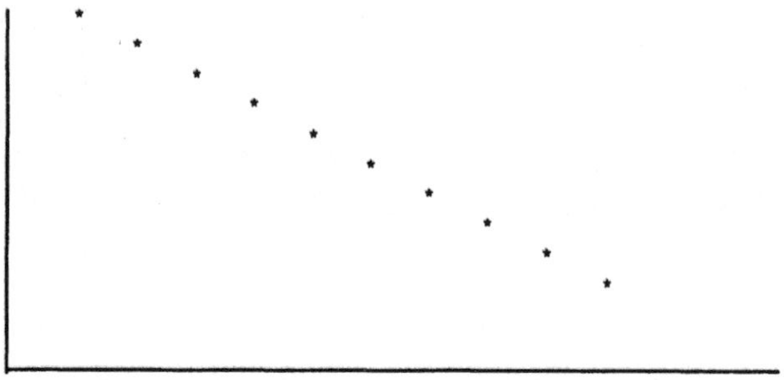

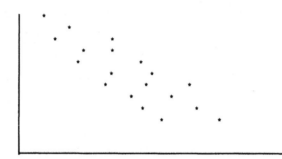

Figure V.10a. Scatter Diagram (Highly Negative)

Figure V.10b. Scatter Diagram (Low to Moderate Negative)

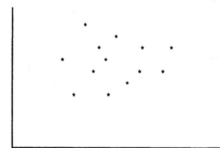

Figure V.10c. Scatter Diagram (Zero Correlation)

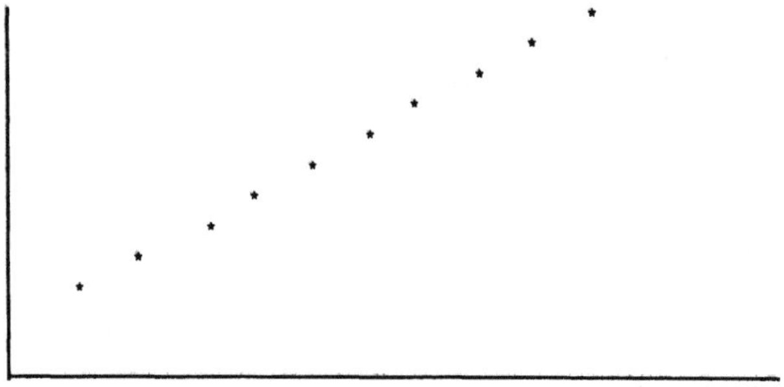

Figure V.10d. Scatter Diagram (Highly Positive)

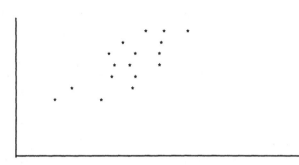

Figure V.10e. Scatter Diagram (Low to Moderate Positive)

"X-Y" chart to determine correlation, i.e., highly positive, positive, no correlation, negative, and highly negative. Figures V.10a through V.10e show the types of scatter diagrams used to determine relationships between data elements.

   Some typical examples of data correlation are the measure of the consumption of fuel for a power plant at several levels of electrical energy output, the cooling of a substance over time, and the loss of efficiency of electrical power tools with reductions in voltage. Scatter diagrams are useful for illustrating the effect or no effect on one variable when the other variable is changed.

Graphs. These diagrams may vary in type from the vertical bar chart to the horizontal bar chart to a pie chart. The purpose is to be able to compare values for analysis to determine the frequency of occurrence, the relationship of information over time, the relative frequency of occurrence of items within a group, or other comparative analysis to reveal or suggest a course of action.

Graphic illustrations are useful to visually show comparative sizes and relationships

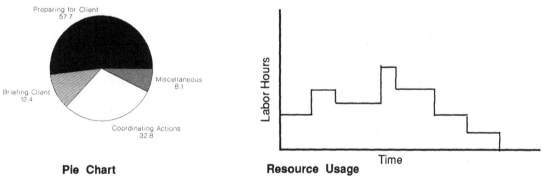

Pie Chart   **Resource Usage**
Figure V.11. Graphs (Sample)

of similar types of data. For example, a budget can be shown in a pie chart to depict allocation of funds to different categories of project work. A second example is the use of a bar chart to show the planned versus actual time required to complete job.

	Number of Times
Marred appearance of enamel	/////////
Inoperative switch	//////
Broken leg	//////
Missing screw(s)	////
Temperature control jammed	////
Incomplete wire connection	////
Damaged electrical plug	///

Figure V.12. Check Sheet (Sample)

Check sheets. These sheets (also called tic sheets) are designed to collect data on specific processes or subprocesses to determine the frequency of occurrence of defined activities. For example, it may be helpful to know the number of times a machine stops during a defined period of time or the number of times an operator leaves a work area to obtain additional materials. These sheets differ from check lists in that this supports a frequency count and a check list is designed to force a discrete response in a block.

Check lists. These are structured lists of items or actions that encompass a process or procedure. The list of items is structured to permit answering the question or statement with a "yes," "no," or "NA" (not applicable) to ensure all elements are checked. This check list approach is designed to force an individual to perform all required elements of a procedure or process before advancing to another function. An excellent example of a check list is the list of items that a pilot uses to ensure positive checking of critical aspects of the aircraft before flight.

	Yes	No	N/A	
Fuel selector set to full tank				
Parking brake on				
Ignition and master switches off				
Cowl flaps open				
Engine induction air - filtered				
Landing gear switch - down				
Mixture control - idle cutoff				
Propeller - high rpm				
Throttle - closed				
Boost pump - off				

Figure V.13. Check List (Sample)

H. Summary

The use of statistical quality processes to improve the quality of a product often is overlooked because the project is thought to be outside the scope of mathematical methods. Because the project is often an integration effort, materials, parts, components, assemblies, and systems acquired from vendors will have a significant affect on the project's end product if inferior items are used. Therefore, an understanding and familiarity with statistical processes provides the ability to validate the vendors to ensure the parts of the project meet the customer's requirements.

The use of the tools of quality management is also essential to the execution of quality programs within a project to provide the greatest degree of assurance that the project's product meets that customer's requirement. These tools assist and support the project manager in the identification of deviations from standards and often provide indications of the courses of action most effective in resolving nonconformances.

The most important resource requiring effective management for the best project results is people. Project people and their individual and collective needs are key to managing this resource group to meet the quality aspects of the project. The identification of individuals or groups of individuals who are components of the project's quality team assists in meeting their needs as "partners" in the project.

Chapter VI   Quality and People in Project Management

A. Introduction

People, more than any other resource, make the difference in quality for a project. The combination and diversity of knowledge, skills, and abilities in the project's participants can affect the planning, implementation, and operation of the product to a greater degree than any other resource. The recruiting, hiring, training, and supervising of individuals and team building for a project are the most crucial aspects of project management.

B. The Capabilities of Project People

Management of people is more than the day-to-day direction of individuals to perform selected tasks, it is the totality of actions that clearly define what is to be done, how it is to be done, when it is to be done, and the standards expected in the final product or service. This necessitates clear policy statement from top management and easily understood requirements and standards. In addition, individuals must understand why the tasks are being done and be willing to meet the standards.

In preparing individuals for the tasks of the project, management must evaluate individual skills and knowledge to ensure that everyone on the project is equipped with the requisite ability to perform at the proper level. In many instances, there will be training and indoctrination requirements to enhance skills and knowledge for project implementation. Training should be structured to enhance or teach new skills, depending upon the level of proficiency required and the individuals' existing skill levels. Indoctrination ranges from initial orientation to the project to a detailed program of the quality requirements for the project.

Of major concern for the project is the use of subcontractors and vendors to provide services to the project. Qualification of individuals is the responsibility of the providing subcontractor or vendor, but the project manager must ensure that the minimum skills, knowledge, and abilities are resident in these individuals. This is accomplished by specifying in the formal contract, purchase order, or other documentation the required skills, knowledge, and abilities to meet the quality requirements.

C. Decision-Performance Options Matrix

Decisions as to the type and amount of work to be accomplished in any project organization is the responsibility of management, while performing it is the responsibility of the team member. This general statement of responsibilities defines management's options for selecting the right as opposed to the wrong tasks/jobs to be accomplished. The second responsibility is for team members to do the work correctly. There are no shades of gray for either the manager or the team member, it is either right or wrong.

The selection of tasks to be accomplished and the performance of work directly affects the end product of a project. If a manager directs the wrong work to be performed, it is of little consequence how well the team member is able to complete the task because it results in a non-contributing task that is done well.

If a manager directs the right work and the team member completes the task improperly, the end result is the right task done below the required standard. The winning solution is achieved only when the manager directs the right work and it is accomplished to standards.

In the implementation of a project, there are many options for the work to be performed. The successful project manager will have the vision to direct and implement the correct type of work to achieve the project's objectives. Less successful projects may have degrees of success in directing and implementing the work to make a profit for the owners or stockholders while achieving customer satisfaction.

It is helpful to view the work in an abstract mode to understand the various options available to a manager. Figure VI.1 depicts the area of feasible solution for all competing alternatives. This is explained as "doing the right (wrong) work" as directed by the manager. The right work is defined as those actions that represent the best interests of the project.

To illustrate the concept, Figure VI.1 shows four possible options. The four boxes represent first the manager's decision as to the work to be accomplished, and second, the team member's performance of the work.

Work to be Accomplished (Manager's Decision)	Job Performance (Team Member)	
	Wrong	Right
Right	Right-Wrong	Right-Right
Wrong	Wrong-Wrong	Wrong-Right

Figure VI.1. Area of Feasible Solution for Quality Work

All project work is tested by the criteria of being "right" or "wrong" for the project's interests. Therefore, the manager should direct work that only meets the criteria for being in the "right," or top half, of the area of feasible solution. Directing the "wrong" work, as represented by the "wrong," or bottom half, of the area of feasible solution, is obviously counter to the project's best interests.

The second part of the area of feasible solution is "doing the work right," or the right side of the box. This is accomplished by the team member after the tasks have been assigned by management. The criteria for doing the task right is that the process conforms to the process specifications and the resulting product conforms to the product specifications. The quality approach is to do the task right the first time. Any task that must be done a second time, or if it fails to meet the requirements or specification, is classified as "wrong," or on the left side of the box.

This simple illustration of the area of feasible solution for task selection and task performance shows the need to develop criteria for management to determine whether a task is included in the project. The capability of a team member to perform the right task is dependent upon the individual's skills, knowledge, abilities, and motivation. Assuring that the team member is prepared to perform the work is a responsibility of management.

An example of management selecting the wrong task is tasking a university for studies to evaluate the state-of-the-art equipment for conducting infrared surveillance. The cost of the study was more than $200,000 and used students under the supervision of a professor. The reports for the study effort were never read or provided the contractor developing the project's product—an infrared surveillance device. The conduct of the study and building the project's product were in parallel. Therefore, the study could not contribute to the project.

D. Management

The primary responsibility for quality rests with the management in a company. Management is responsible for selecting the correct strategies for building the company's base and for implementing the correct procedures to fabricate a safe, usable product that meets all the requirements of the customer. Only management has the authority, latitude, and capability to create the environment for the development of a viable product.

These responsibilities for building a quality product rest primarily with management, 85 percent, while the responsibility of the team members is 15 percent. The disparity between the team members' responsibilities for quality and that of the management reflects the need to focus on first improving management's understanding of quality management as a means of improving quality products or services.

Training and indoctrination of senior managers in the principles of quality and the need for continuous improvement is essential to the future well-being of a company. Company managers and project managers must understand the reasons for quality programs and support those efforts through actions. Standards of quality must be established for managers to use as quantitative measures of progress. Efforts must be focused on prevention, not correction of defects. Measures of quality should be in financial terms as a common base and include such defect results as waste, rework, additional materials, and additional time. Most of all, managers must be sensitive to customer requirements and how those requirements translate to the company or project.

E. Team Members

Team members are assigned work to accomplish and most often given procedures to follow in the implementation of the work. Currently, management often assumes that the team member fully understands the work (has knowledge of the procedures and requirements), has the skills to perform the work, and is motivated to perform at a superior level. This often is not the situation in fast moving projects where managers have little time to communicate the requirements.

To ensure a quality orientation, the team member can only assume responsibility for meeting the requirements of completing the work when he/she:

- Knows what is expected to meet the specifications.
- Knows how to perform the functions to meet the specifications.
- Has adequate tools to perform the function.
- Is able to measure performance during the process.
- Is able to adjust the process to match the desired outcome.

In addition to being equipped with the knowledge, skills, and ability, the team member must understand the reason for completing work in a prescribed fashion. This indoctrination with the reasons for correctly performing the procedure does not permit deviation through finding an easier method or one assumed to meet the requirements. The team members must, however, be empowered to act in situations that are within their scope of knowledge.

Team members trained in the procedures must receive refresher training to maintain skills and receive selected training to improve skills for new processes or technology. They must be given the tools to perform the assigned tasks as well as the skills to perform the work. The type and quantity of tools provided to the operators can make a significant difference in the end product built by the team members.

F. Quality Team for a Project

The quality team, or partners in quality, for the project are senior management, the project manager, the project staff, the customer, vendors and suppliers, subcontractors, and the public at large as represented by the regulatory authorities. Each plays a vital role in the quality of projects either by their active or passive conduct at various times during the planning, implementation, operation and maintenance, or close-out of a project. The quality role of all parties is more of a partnership than a team effort because of the return on investment to each, based on their contributions. Figure VI.2 shows the relationships between these partners in quality.

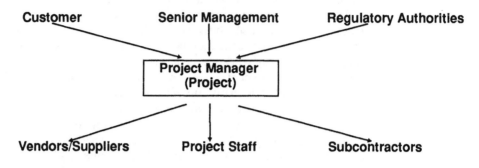

Figure VI.2. Partners in Project Quality

The integration of all quality participants centers around the project and is the responsibility of the project manager. Contractual relationships, whether formal documents, purchase orders, or informal agreements, must be established between the participants to ensure a mutual understanding of the customer's requirements and the ability to meet those requirements. These contractual commitments are enforced by the project manager and the project team during the implementation phase.

Customer

The customer is key to the quality function of the project because the customer sets the requirements. The requirements, however, must be achievable, stable, and unambiguous. Achievable requirements mean the end product of the project can be accomplished within the time, resource, and stated technical parameters. Stable requirements are well-developed statements of the product or service to be provided by the project. The requirements should not be frequently changed during the planning and implementation of the project, though some change of design and method may occur. Unambiguous requirements can only be interpreted one way to permit the development of specifications, drawings, designs, and statements of work for the project. Furthermore, the requirements must be mutually understood by all project participants.

The customer also plays a key role in project quality during design reviews, progress reviews, and at key milestones in the schedule. The progress of planning and working on the project may require a decision of the customer at these points when unexpected activities occur. The customer's timely decision is required to ensure the continuation or redirection of work on the project without a significant loss of momentum or resources.

Project Manager

The project manager is the focal point for ensuring all quality functions are established and implemented during the life of the project. As the focal point, the project manager translates the customer's requirements into specifications and statements of work to ensure the requirements will be met, i.e., conform to the requirements. Next is implementation of the specifications and statements of work in a manner that causes the project team to meet all the requirements. Checks and audits during and after the project execution are conducted by the project manager to determine whether the requirements are being met.

Essential to the quality function is the continuous coordination and information exchange between the project manager and the customer. The project manager must take the initiative to keep the customer informed of project progress and any situations that could impact project quality, i.e., cost, schedule, or technical performance. When there is a change to the design of the system or plan, the project manager must negotiate the change with the customer—to the customer's satisfaction. The changes resulting from negotiation will alter the project's baseline and cause the redirection of resources.

Senior Management

Quality management at the project level works only when it is an extension of corporate policy and procedures. Senior management must establish and maintain an active quality program in the corporation that extends to projects as each is planned and implemented. Senior management provides the base for the project's quality program, which is tailored to the unique aspects of the individual project.

Senior management for the project plays a vital role in supporting the project manager's requests for critical and qualified resources to perform work. When operating in a matrix environment, the project manager at times requires increased priority to meet the quality requirements of the project. Trained, knowledgeable people are necessary to accomplish the work. Senior management must provide these resources through setting priorities and directing activities that support the project.

Vendors and Suppliers

Vendors and suppliers of parts, components, systems, and materials are an integral part of the quality team. These partners in the quality process respond to requests/orders for elements of the project product with either conforming or nonconforming inputs. The hierarchy of project and first and second level vendors/suppliers is depicted in Figure VI.3.

The capability of the first level vendor/supplier to provide conforming materials and parts is dependent upon the second level of supplier/vendor. Therefore, the first level vendor/supplier must have the capability to determine whether the inputs to the system meet quality specifications. In turn, the project manager must have the capability to determine whether the first level vendors/suppliers are meeting the requirements of the project. In meeting this

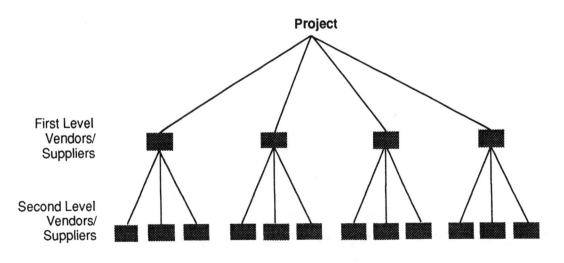

Figure VI.3. Hierarchy of Vendors/Suppliers

responsibility, the project manager must have knowledge of statistical process control techniques, acceptance sampling, and sampling techniques.

Subcontractors

Subcontractors provide materials, components, assemblies, and integration services to the project's system. Of concern to the quality function of the project and vital to the overall project quality, the subcontractors execute parts of the contract for the project manager. This execution of the contract, although through a contractual document between the project and the subcontractor, must conform to the requirements the same as if the work was performed by the project staff. Thus, subcontractors must understand the requirements as defined in specifications and statements of work to ensure the work is performed in a manner that provides confidence in the outcome.

Subcontractors' quality policies and procedures will often differ from the project's corporate program. Any differences should be resolved during the subcontractor selection process and negotiated to ensure each subcontractor will be capable of performing at the required level. The contracts between the project and the subcontractors must flow down all the requirements of the project's contract with the customer for an assigned portion of the work. It is the responsibility of the project manager to ensure all requirements are included in the specification and statement of work for the subcontractor.

Regulatory Authorities

Regulatory authorities interpret and implement the laws in the form of directives. These directives have the effect of the law and impose detailed requirements on projects, depending upon project type and affected environment. Regulatory authorities are responsible for such areas as radio frequency management, ecological changes, and nuclear safety.

Project managers must identify these "customers" and their requirements so that regulatory needs are anticipated and included in the planning. Failure to meet regulatory requirements can adversely affect projects, with delays in approvals to proceed, rework to meet minimum requirements, or cancellation of the project because of the inability to meet the requirements within schedule and budget constraints for the subcontractor.

Project Staff

The project staff are resources, but must also be considered customers in the sense that the expectations of the staff include conflict resolution, clear direction, decisive action, and leadership from the project manager. A project manager's failure to meet the expectations (requirements) of the staff results in lower productivity and probably a lower level of project success than the project manager who meets the staff's expectations. Another result of failure to meet the staff's expectation is rapid personnel turnover in an already temporary situation.

Project managers should manage the project staff as a group rather than attempt to manage individuals. The focus on team building and group dynamics will provide greater return in managing the staff and meeting their expectations. There are occasions, however, when individuals do not respond to team building efforts and group dynamics. It is the project manager's responsibility to provide counseling on an individual basis to unite this individual with the staff as a supporting team member.

G. Quality Project Team Development

Development of a quality project team is the responsibility of the project manager. Because a project is the systematic building of tasks, the focus of team building is not on any particular group of individuals or the team as a whole, but is a system of three categories for management.

Reviews and Audits

The project manager conducts reviews and audits of the project to monitor and direct the quality level of the work. Following are key reviews and audits supporting the development of a team.

Management reviews of project work determine the status, progress made since the last review, problems with ongoing work, and solutions to problems. These are held on a weekly, monthly, or quarterly basis, depending upon the perceived need for monitoring the project's activities and the complexity of the project.

Peer reviews of selected project work determine whether proposed or completed work meets the requirements. These reviews, performed by a group of peers, are useful in evaluating research and development work because of the lack of an historical data base for reference. Peer reviews are normally ad hoc meetings to address specific problems.

Competency center reviews are conducted by organizations with a reputation for excellence in the area of competency. These reviews are used to validate documentation, studies, and propose technical solutions to problems. The Center may be asked to visit a project site or conduct the review from its facilities.

Fitness reviews and audits are measures to determine the fitness of a product or part of a project. The review is usually a meeting to discuss the relative merits of the item being addressed. The audit is a more detailed examination of the product, documentation, practices, procedures, and processes, as appropriate, to determine the relative fitness of the project or product. Conducted on an ad hoc basis, these audits address specific issues.

Managing the Process

Managing the project process is directing actions and measuring the results of those actions.

Staff meetings are designed to exchange information between participants to ensure a coordinated effort on the project. Decisions may be announced, actions given to individuals, general policy changes announced, and ongoing activities discussed. The focus of each meeting is on short-term activities to promote better understanding of an immediate situation. Staff meetings are usually scheduled once a week. Care must be exercised to prioritize agenda items to ensure the proper items are discussed and all participants are well prepared.

Steering committee is a group of senior managers who provide guidance for the general direction of the project from a more generic prospective. The committee does not usually become involved in daily activities, but will provide broad guidance for the longer term. Steering committees are used for long-term projects, joint ventures, and high-risk, complex projects.

Performance measurement system measures the progress of a project. It is an indicator of whether the project is progressing as planned or whether there is a deviation from the planned baseline. The most common system being used is the Earned-Value System, or Cost-Schedule Control System.

Achievement recognition is a means of rewarding individuals or groups for meeting or exceeding requirements. An awards program recognizes behavior that builds on the project's success and promotes similar behavior from other individuals or groups. This is a most effective means of building morale among a project team.

Communications

Effective communication between and among the project team is the best method of promoting an understanding of the work requirements and quality orientation for all. Communications should use many different media to effectively convey messages and information about the project and its requirements.

Documentation includes the project budget, charter, configuration plan, drawings, sketches, implementation plan, and other written media. All project documents are media for communicating project requirements.

Meetings may be regularly scheduled or ad hoc gatherings of individuals to conduct oral exchanges. Exchange of information in this manner may be formal meetings with minutes or may be informal coordination of specific items.

Organization charts are used to show reporting relationships, coordination relationships, and matrix arrangements for specific resources or services. These charts may also depict the responsibilities of individuals as an addendum.

Work standards describe parametric values that must be achieved for work, procedures for performing a task or activity, and safety requirements and prohibitions that must be observed. Work standards provide a uniform basis for work accomplishment.

H. Summary

People are crucial to accomplishing work in a timely and cost-effective manner. Similarly, people are vital to building quality into a project's product. The combination of human resources, or the quality team, contributes essential ingredients that must meld together in a conciliatory fashion to meet the customer's requirements. While the project manager is viewed as one who orchestrates the project, each contributor from the vendor/supplier to the craftsman to the customer plays a critical role in quality management.

Management is generally considered to be responsible for 85 percent or more of those factors influencing quality of a product. The key to management's role is making decisions and communicating about what is the "right work" to be performed. This direction of the "right work" is derived from the goals and objectives of the project and whether the work is supportive of these goals and objectives. Management must also ensure the availability of the right tools, right methods, and right systems for performing the right work.

The team member is charged with implementing the directions of management to perform all work in the "right manner," i.e., conforming to the customer's requirements. The conduct of this work in the "right manner" assumes that the team member has the knowledge, skills, abilities, and motivation to perform the work as well as having the authority to change a process that is wrong. These team member attributes are screened by the project manager during the planning phase and prior to project implementation to ensure that resources meet the performance requirements. The team member must be provided tools to properly perform the work to standards.

The development and maintenance of a quality project team requires the use of several methods and tools for building relationships. These methods and tools should be used by the project manager in planning, implementing, and closing a project. The combination and frequency of use is dependent upon the project environment, the project manager's management style, and the composition of the project quality team.

Using an example of a project and its quality building process reflects some actual situations that can occur in the implementation of a project quality program. This actual situation, with the names changed and the time span condensed, reflects some potential pitfalls that one may experience. The example has been modified to provide a smooth flow while reflecting only the details necessary to promote understanding.

Chapter VII   Achieving Project Quality

A. Projects and Quality

Infusing quality into projects is achievable through a dedicated effort of setting standards for the work, understanding the customer's requirements, and implementing the requirements in all documentation and actions. Quality is achieved through planning, directing, and implementing actions that are consistent with the concept of *do the right thing right the first time.* Using the tools of modern quality management to monitor, evaluate, and assess the processes while conducting continuous improvement in the processes is the foundation for achieving quality.

The initial efforts are focused on understanding the customer's requirements and achieving a mutual understanding of the technical approach to meeting these requirements. The project manager is the prime mover in bringing about this mutual understanding through analysis of the customer's stated and implied requirements to develop the implementation plan. The customer's expectations are set by the project implementation plan and any initial briefings provided by the project manager.

Some organizations conduct a mutual understanding conference for projects prior to signing the contract. The conference provides the opportunity for questions, answers, and clarifications of the proposed contract. Any clarifications are incorporated into the contractual documents prior to contract award. This may delay the start of the project while statements of work, specifications, terms and conditions, and other aspects are amended. The final contract, however, is less subject to change during the implementation phase and the project team will have a better definition of the requirements for planning.

Preparing well-structured plans for the project, based on the customer's requirements, permits anticipation of the course of work and the degree of difficulty involved in implementing each major part of the project. The identification and allocation of resources appropriate to meeting the requirements well in advance of the implementation allows time to schedule and position them prior to their need. The plans also form a baseline which can be reviewed as guidance for the project and the basis for making changes when necessary.

During implementation, the project may be an extension of an organization or it may be the company in its entirety. The policies and procedures for quality must flow down from the parent organization as they apply to projects. The human resources can be expected to respond to quality on a project the same as they would in the parent organization. Weaknesses in corporate quality programs can be expected to migrate into projects. Therefore, projects, as temporary efforts, must rely on the parent organization to instill many of the quality practices in the assigned individuals prior to project initiation.

The project manager has a major responsibility to maintain contact with the customer to monitor the need for change as well as keeping the customer informed of progress. Periodic meetings for briefing the customer and receiving feedback on the customer's concurrence or nonconcurrence with the report of progress are important considerations in managing the direction of the project. The customer's confidence in the project manager is often directly related to how well the customer is kept informed and the project manager's ability to adjust the flow of work to meet the customer's expectations.

Quality is the combination of meeting the customer's requirements for the end product of the project, keeping the customer informed of the progress, and being able to change the course of work to meet emerging requirements. The project manager must be proactive in managing the relationship with the customer through establishing a working relationship that facilitates the exchange of information and permits latitude in implementation of project work while meeting the technical specifications.

B. Modern Quality Management Applied to Projects

Project managers need to understand the concepts of statistical control and the tools available to identify defects for corrective actions. The collection of quantitative data for statistical analysis is the basis for proactive management by *fact* rather than management by *exception*. Management by fact is the use of data to give indications of the correctness of processes or the deviation from the required standard. Management by exception is the observation of errors or defects before any action is taken. Management by exception lets errors and defects happen before management intervention.

The current thrust in quality management is the prevention of defects through a program of selecting the proper materials, training and indoctrinating people, and planning a process that ensures the appropriate outcome. This requires an investment in training people with the skills needed to perform at the expected level and indoctrination of people with the knowledge of why quality is important. Designing a project process during the planning phase, with all the forward-reaching prevention measures, sets the stage for a successful implementation.

Following the plan and adjusting as necessary to meet the customer's requirements during implementation are keys to a quality project. Any change from the plan should be based on sound requirements and must be documented to provide the audit trail of activities for post-project evaluation. This documenting of change, or amendment to the project plan, is necessary to ensure subsequent projects benefit from the updated procedures.

C. Project Quality Example

This example uses a simulated high-technology company that produces electro-optic devices in support of computer, telecommunications, and cablevision markets. All products are components or parts to facilitate the transmission of information between computers, electronic telephone switches, and television stations and television sets. Products are unique in their design and functions for different applications, but use the same electro-optic technology. [1]

The Delta Three Company has bid on a contract to produce 5,000 light modulators that convert electronic signals to light waves for transmission over fiber-optic cable. The light modulators will be identical in size and performance. The modulators are unique end products that must be built to customer requirements.

Decision to Use Project Management

Delta's management decides to use project management principles and techniques to direct the modulator work in a new building located two miles from the corporate headquarters. The project manager is appointed because of his education and experience in the light modulator field. A deputy project manager and a project control team is assigned. Contract administration, financial management, purchasing, and the technicians for assembling the modulators will be provided on an as-required basis from corporate functional areas.

Management has also directed the project manager to implement quality management as a major effort in improving productivity at the lowest cost. Because Delta bid the project at a fixed price with half the margin of the electronics industry to win the work, there is little latitude for delays in schedule, rework, waste of materials, or end product failures. Corporate will absorb all costs for new skills training and capital expenses to change the current system. The project budget must include all expenses directly related to product planning, design, and build.

Product Specification

The specifications for the modulator are as follows.

Fabricate, test and deliver 5,000 light modulators that will convert computer data signals to light signals for transmission over fiber-optic cables. Each modulator will be capable of converting 256 electronic signals to a similar, discrete number of modulated light signals. The specific parameters for the modulator are:

- Power use: 110 or 120 VAC
- Maximum size: 4x5x2 inches
- Frequency: 25 GHz plus or minus 100 Hz
- Reliability: disposable after a life of ten years
- Durability: withstand shock of 1.5 Gs
- Maintainability: disposable
- External cover: paint gray enamel
- Marking: serially number each modulator and label each with the product identification number; use a bar code for scanning to facilitate inventory control
- Environment: installed on the back of a computer; must sustain temperature ranges of 20 to 120 degrees Fahrenheit and humidity levels up to 80 percent
- Documentation: contractor to provide instructions for connecting the modulator to the computer and test procedures for assuring the proper connection; one set of instructions for each modulator

Financial Analysis

The projected budget for the light modulator contract is shown in Figure VII.1. Two budgets have been developed for the project.

The financial officer is aware of the current predictions of productivity improvement through quality approaches to managing work and has computed the budget at two levels of efficiency. The records for wasted material and extra labor to correct defects reflect an increase in costs by 10.37 percent. Senior management believes waste can be reduced to 1 percent of the direct costs for both material and labor.

The financial officer computes the first budget at 14 percent waste of materials and labor for a total profit of $165,831. The second budget uses 3 percent waste in materials and labor for a total profit of $352,220. This savings of 11 percent in materials and labor more than doubles the profit. Another way to view the financial aspect of the change in productivity is profit as a percent of sales. For the 14 percent productivity loss, the sales-profit contribution is 3.9 percent. For the 3 percent loss in productivity, the sales-profit contribution is 8.3 percent.

In view of senior management's desire to bid at a low margin, the only means of improving the profit picture is by increasing productivity with a quality management approach. The project manager is challenged to implement the quality program which will achieve 6 percent profit through reduced waste. Six percent profit is viewed as a reasonable goal for the initial quality management effort.

Planning for Quality

The project manager assesses the contract and documentation to evaluate the customer's requirements. It is noted that a mutual understanding conference was

DELTA THREE CORPORATION
(Budget at 86% Productivity)

Item	Qtr 1	Qtr 2	Qtr 3	Qtr 4	Yr Total
Sales	422,500	1,267,500	1,690,000	845,000	4,255,000
Units	500	1,500	2,000	1,000	5,000
Raw Material	66,860	200,581	267,442	133,721	668,604
Labor	273,547	820,640	1,094,186	547,093	2,735,466
Overhead	54,012	153,036	202,548	103,524	513,120
Total Cost	394,419	1,174,257	1,564,176	784,338	3,917,190
Gross Margin	28,081	93,243	125,824	60,662	307,810
Taxes @ 50%	14,041	46,622	62,912	30,331	153,905
Net Profit	14,041	46,622	62,912	30,331	153,905
% of Sales	3.3%	3.7%	3.7%	3.6%	3.6%

DELTA THREE CORPORATION
(Budget at 97% Productivity)

Item	Qtr 1	Qtr 2	Qtr 3	Qtr 4	Yr Total
Sales	422,500	1,267,500	1,690,000	845,000	4,255,000
Units	500	1,500	2,000	1,000	5,000
Raw Material	59,278	177,835	237,113	118,557	592,783
Labor	242,526	727,577	970,103	485,052	2,425,258
Overhead	48,397	136,191	180,089	92,294	456,971
Total Cost	350,201	1,041,603	1,387,305	605,903	3,475,012
Gross Margin	72,299	225,897	302,695	149,097	749,988
Taxes @ 50%	36,150	112,949	151,348	74,549	374,994
Net Profit	36,150	112,949	151,348	74,549	374,994
% of Sales	8.6%	8.9%	9.0%	8.8%	8.9%

Figure VII.1. Light Modulator Project Budget

held with the customer to assure all parts of the contract were understood. Two items were resolved during the conference: (1) the delivery schedule for the modulators is as reflected in the budget and (2) payment for the modulators will be within thirty days following each delivery.

a. Process. The project manager uses the process reverse flow for developing the product's inputs. The description of the end product is decomposed into material, personnel, method, time, energy, machine, measurement, and environment requirements. Although the modulators will be built by progressive line mode in a large batch by a standardized process, the planning will be for a single modulator and then expanded to the total requirement of 5,000 units. The inputs for each category are as follows.

Material. Substrate, polymer, container, solder, screws, light source, RC 232 electrical connector, fiber-optic cable connector.

Personnel. One physicist, five polymer technicians, two assemblers, one tester, one product scheduler/project controller, one administrative assistant, one deputy project manager, one project manager.

Method. Delta Standard 10-3 (Polymer Spincoating Standards and Procedures), Delta Standard 10-7 (Modulator Assembly Standards and Procedures),

Delta Standard 10-23 (Standard Tests for Modulators: Thermal, Shock, Electrical Cycling, and Humidity), Delta Standard 10-24 (Tests of Light Waveguides), Delta Standard 10-29 (Workmanship Standards), and Delta Standard 10-31 (Standard and Frequency for Precision Machine Calibration).

Time. Contract specifies one year after contract award to deliver all 5,000 units. See schedule of work for details.

Energy. All energy requirements are for electrical power to light facilities, operate air-conditioning, operate clean rooms, and operate machines and tools. The cost of energy is included in overhead cost projections.

Machine. Five soldering irons, one modulator test stand, one thermal oven, five assembly jigs, two clean rooms, five assembly benches, one spincoating machine, two substrate cutters, and one container sealing machine.

Measurement. Initial and monthly calibration required for modulator test stand, thermal oven temperature gauges, spincoating machine. See Delta Standard 10-31 (Standard and Frequency for Precision Machine Calibration).

Environment. Spincoating and substrate assembly to be accomplished in a Class 10 clean room; all other work accomplished at facility temperature (65 to 72 degrees Fahrenheit) and no humidity control.

During the review of the Delta Standards, the project manager did not find a procedure for the identification and correction of defects or problems. He developed the following procedure.

b. **Concurrent engineering.** The project manager recognizes the need to design and build the modulators in a relatively short time to meet the initial delivery

---

DELTA STANDARD 10-( )
(Problem Identification and Resolution Procedures)

When a problem is identified within a project, the initial reaction is to correct the defect and not necessarily be concerned with the "root cause" of the problem. For example, an improper assembly of a part to the component is viewed as a problem of needing to rework and assemble the part. This action will bring the defective assembly operation into conformance with the customer's requirement. The true problem is why and how did the improper assembly occur.

The method for corrective action is a five-step operation that includes correcting the immediate defect, identifying root causes, adjusting the process, and conducting follow-up to ensure the problem has been corrected. Also, the follow-up evaluates the process to ensure other parameters have not been affected to create new defects. The sequence of actions are outlined below.

Define the problem. Defining includes characterizing the problem to ensure all aspects are covered and establishing a measure of when the problem is corrected. Identifying and collecting the proper resources is essential to having the capability to effect the corrective actions.

Fix the problem. Using the identified resources, initiate corrective actions and record the completed actions with the costs to fix the problem.

Identify the root causes. Conduct a thorough examination of the problem within the context of the process. Examine the design, audit the workmanship, and inspect the measuring instrument precision. Identify the defect in the process that allows the problem to occur.

Take corrective actions. Using the information derived from the evaluation of root causes, correct the process by using a new design, adjusting the current process, or conducting training. Implement phased process controls to ensure a revised process can be evaluated at internal check points.

Evaluate and follow up. Conduct periodic follow-up of the corrective actions to ensure measures implemented are effective and have corrected the root cause of the problems.

---

requirement of 500 units during the first quarter. It is planned to use project scheduling techniques to plan and display the activities of the customer, engineering, and production.

The project manager will hold a conference on concurrent engineering with the customer, engineering, and production. The conference will more fully develop the requirement in concrete terms to permit design of a product that specifically meets the customer's requirements. Engineering will ask questions to clarify all design needs and provide feedback on their ability to meet the customer's requirements. Production will anticipate the producibility of the modulator in lots of 100, 1000, and 2000.

Following the initial conference, engineering will prepare detailed drawings and manufacturing specifications. Production, in cooperation with engineering, will lay out the job shop to ensure a smooth flow of work. As soon as the initial drawings and specifications are complete, production will build five prototypes for testing and demonstration. The prototype build will also validate the process capability and identify any defects in the process flow.

The second conference will be to review the drawings and specifications with the customer and demonstrate any completed prototypes. Based on the customer's agreement as to the drawings and specifications, production will take the lead to initiate the manufacturing of modulators. A third conference may be required if the customer does not agree to the drawings and specifications. This would delay the production schedule.

Once production has started the manufacturing process, engineering will monitor the technical progress and assist with any producibility issues. The project manager will keep the customer informed as to the progress and anticipated delivery schedules. (See Figure VII.2.)

c. **Schedule.** The schedule depicts the time-dependent plan for conducting activities to meet the delivery schedule.

d. **Training and indoctrination.** The skill levels of all participants meets the minimum and no new hires are anticipated for this project. The project team, however, has not been provided the quality briefing and quality requirements

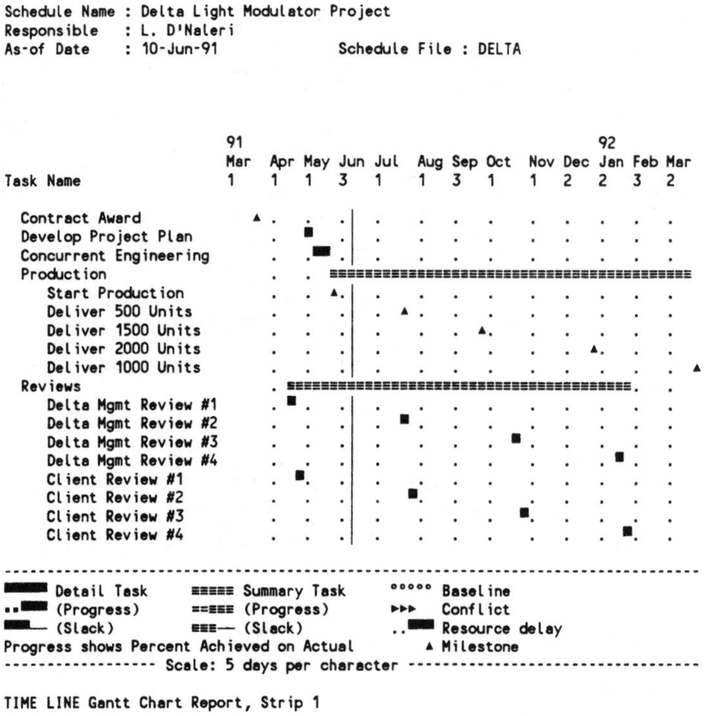

Figure VII.2. Light Modulator Schedule

orientation. Corporate must conduct the quality briefings and quality requirements orientation prior to implementation of the project. The briefings will include details of the Delta Standards and the requirement to adhere to the proven methods.

The project manager has taken a course on quality through the local university night school and will use some of the material during the kickoff meeting to introduce the theme "Customer Satisfaction: Defect-Free Products." The project manager will set the goal of defect-free products by doing all work right the first time.

e. **Facilities layout.** The project manager seeks the advice and assistance of the engineering department to lay out the flow of work to ensure there is minimum disruption of the work flow. There is also an evaluation of the human factors for the working environment. Stools are available, workbenches are the correct height, light intensity is optimized for the type of work, and rubber mats are on the floor to cushion feet. The electrostatic discharge ground wires are installed. Rest rooms and a break area for eating are easily accessible to all workers. Signs designating restricted areas and safety rules are conspicuously posted. Visitor control procedures are in effect to restrict work areas to authorized persons.

Implementation

The project manager conducts the kickoff meeting with the theme for quality, "Customer Satisfaction: Defect Free Products." Figure VII.3 is used to explain to the workers the process by which the modulators will be designed, built, and delivered to the customer.

a. **Concurrent engineering.** The project manager successfully conducts the meeting between the customer, engineering, and production to reach an agreement on the customer's requirements and the schedule for draft drawings and specifications. Agreement to the final requirements and detailed

---

REQUIREMENT: 5,000 Delta light modulators
Connect computers to fiber-optic cable
Data rate of 25 GHz
Installation and operating instructions

SPECIFICATION: See engineering drawings

APPROACH: Set up a progressive line
Work passes from person to person
Testing of light waveguides and modulators*
Environmental testing conducted on each
    lot and with any change of the process
Attach label
Package modulators in lots of 25
Ship lots via rail and truck
Follow up with customer to ensure receipt,
    understanding of instructions, and
    proper installation/operation

* Testing of light waveguide is required before further work or assembly because spincoating technology yields between 65 and 90 percent using existing techniques. Functional testing of all modulators is a low-cost effort to ensure the proper operation of each unit.

Figure VII.3. Key Elements of Light Modulator Project

---

specifications is reached during the second meeting, with production demonstrating three of the five prototypes. Two prototypes failed the bench test procedures; one showed response rates of less than 2.3 KHz against a requirement of 25 GHz while the second gave no response to an electrical stimulation (apparently a break in the electrical or optical chain).

b. **Delta management review.** A briefing is given by the project manager on the status of the project, with specific details on the failure of the two modulators. It is the project manager's belief that the 60 percent yield in good modulators (prototypes) is indicative of the future. This low yield will result in a major cost overrun. A precise estimate cannot be made based on a run of five modulators. The two defective modulators and the engineering notebooks were reviewed by the design engineers. One modulator had a faulty light waveguide, which was caused by dirt in the polymer, and the second modulator had an improper alignment between the waveguide and the optical chain. The dirt in the polymer could have been contaminated material from the supplier or introduced during the spincoating process. The alignment of the waveguide and optic chain is either improper workmanship or tools (jigs).

Management directs the project manager to resolve the low yield issue and immediately start production of the modulators. The schedule is in jeopardy if there is any delay.

c. **Corrective measures.** The project manager determines that they do not have sufficient knowledge and skills to maintain the level of cleanliness required for the polymer spincoating operation and for the assembly operation to preclude errors in connecting the waveguide to the optic chain. Corrective measures will include four hours of technical training in workmanship standards, assembly procedures, and cleanliness standards.

These measures are implemented, but the project manager knows that small errors of the type identified are indicative of larger problems which will surface later in the project. Therefore, he establishes a Process Improvement Program based on the Process Improvement Cycle Analysis depicted in Figure VII.4.

All units will be serially numbered and defects reported against the unit number. Control charts will be used at the waveguide assembly test stand, final assembly, and unit test bench. All incoming material will be inspected to ensure compliance with acceptance standards. Check sheets will be used to count the types of defects. Standard procedures must be available to the workers.

The deputy project manager will conduct the analyses of data using Pareto diagrams, histograms, and event logs. Any problem identified will be addressed with the procedures outlined in Delta Standard 10-( ) (Problem Identification and Resolutions Procedures) and the cause and effect diagram. All defects will focus on the root cause and a permanent method of resolution. The deputy project manager will conduct a weekly review of the defects found and the problem resolutions for all project team members.

d. **Production phase.** The production phase is initiated and the flow of work is going well when a visual inspection is made of the production facilities. The first two briefings by the deputy project manager have been extremely helpful in showing individuals why work standards are important. The yield for the waveguides is at 87 percent and all bad waveguides are scrap. To protect the technology, all bad waveguides must be destroyed by fire—a cost to dispose of the waste. End product yield is currently 93.6 percent, not counting the scrap waveguides in the end product figures.

The less than optimum yield has reduced production to an estimated 430 at the end of the first quarter as compared to a planned 500 units. The cost per completed unit is running 54.6 percent more than planned because of the scrap and additional number of waveguides being produced. Pareto diagrams show the waveguide to be the most frequent source of defects—72.3 percent of the total defects for the past week.

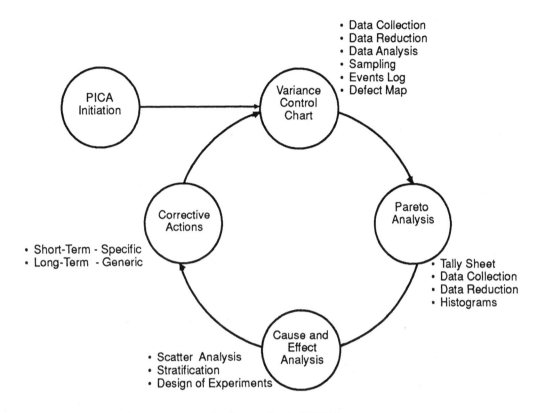

Figure VII.4. Process Improvement Cycle Analysis (PICA)

A review of the control charts show the waveguides to be cycling, or the pattern is one of the parameters transitioning from near the three-sigma upper control limit to near the three-sigma lower control limit. A complete review of the control charts and data shows some significant defects in the process.

First, the control chart was established by incorrectly using upper and lower control limits with a standard deviation value of 1.1, when it should have been 1.001. This increased range allowed the data point at the extreme limits to be accepted as the process being in control. An estimate of the out of control data points appears to be 10 to 14 percent because of the hugging of the upper and lower data points of the cycles.

Second, the cycling of the data points to the extremes is unusual when the procedures are stable and workmanship standards are rigorously adhered to. The logs show the names of individuals working on waveguides who have not attended the quality training classes. Further investigation reveals these individuals are replacements for regular team members on sick leave, vacation, and other absences. Replacements are automatically assigned from the corporate labor pool because of the priority that senior management has assigned to the light modulator project.

The control charts were corrected and both the regular team and replacement individuals were given training in the waveguide fabrication process. A review of the work process procedures showed a dual interpretation. The wording was changed to avoid ambiguous statements and diagrams were added for clarity. Supervisors were instructed to allow only qualified personnel to work on the waveguides.

Defects in the waveguide were immediately reduced to 11 percent of the total defects in the Pareto diagram. Most defects were now in the assembly of the modulators and the existing process showed a yield of 97 percent, or 3 percent defects.

The project manager recognized the problem to be one of process capability falling short. With the tools available, the precision could not be improved for connecting the waveguide to the optic chain. The engineering department was requested to assist in developing a new process or renting a robotic machine that could give precision to the process.

During the first project review, the project manager briefed the customer on the problems of obtaining sufficient yield to meet delivery dates. He explained all the actions being taken to improve the yield and that deliveries, thus far, met all customer expectations in terms of performance. Upon questioning, the customer admitted that some of the 500 units could be delivered a month later than scheduled. A new schedule was negotiated two weeks prior to the contracted delivery date.

e. **Post-project review.** The project manager prepared a report of activities following project completion. He noted that the first-quarter delivery of 500 units fell short by 125 units because of the defects in the initial lots. Negotiating a new schedule with the customer for the initial 500 units was easy because the customer was not surprised at a late date.

The lessons learned included:

- Training was required for all managers and workers to provide a strong corporate quality program.
- The corporate base for quality was not supportive of the project during planning and implementation.
- Being familiar with the tools of modern quality management from the start would have avoided such errors as improper control chart variances and late initiation of process improvement cycle analysis.
- A slow start in using the tools and applying them for the best results cost the project additional funds.

The budget was based on a perfect situation where productivity started at 97 percent. There were no preparatory actions to ensure the yield would be this high, nor is this the case in actual practice. An active quality program would have reduced the impact on the budget and improved the profit margin. It should be noted that the last quarter of the project resulted in a productivity of 98.2 percent because of the quality initiatives and the well-trained, stable work force for that period.

D. Summary

The project must rely on the parent organization to provide the basics of a quality program, especially the policies, procedures, standards, and skill training. The pace of the project does not normally allow the time or resources to conduct a quality orientation and prepare detailed requirements. Individuals working on a project will perform in the same manner and level of workmanship as in previous assignments. Therefore, a change of skill level or knowledge must be accomplished before assignment to the project.

Most projects can benefit from the tools of modern quality management where rapid identification and resolution of problems can be the only way a project can make a profit. Preparing project managers, supervisors and workers to use these tools will facilitate the flow of work through fewer disruptions and more rapid resolution of root cause problems. Most of all, a well-planned quality program can lead to improved productivity levels and better profit margins for corporations while building on customer satisfaction.

---

1. This example is a composite of two projects on which the author consulted and developed the basis for the conduct of work. The names of both companies have been changed or omitted and all information has been changed to protect the proprietary information provided the author.

Appendices

The Japanese Deming Prize (Overseas) Check List provides the criteria for award of this honor. It provides a list of those items which are considered important by the Japanese in their quality program and program for recognition of companies outside Japan. The check list could be used to audit company quality programs without competing for the award.

Appendix A
Deming Prize (Overseas) Check List

1. Policy

How the policy for management, quality and quality control is determined and transmitted throughout all sectors of the company will be examined together with the results being achieved. Whether the contents of the policy are appropriate and clearly presented will also be examined.

a. Policies pursued for management, quality and quality control
b. Method of establishing policies
c. Justifiability and consistency of policies
d. Utilization of statistical methods
e. Transmission and diffusion of policies
f. Review of policies and the results achieved
g. Relationship between policies and long- and short-term planning

2. Organizational Structure

Whether the scope of responsibility and authority is clearly defined, how cooperation is promoted among all departments, and how the organization is managed to carry out quality control will be examined.

a. Explicitness of the scopes of authority and responsibility
b. Appropriateness of delegations of authority
c. Interdivisional cooperation
d. Committees and their activities
e. Utilization of staff
f. Utilization of QC Circle activities
g. Quality control diagnosis

3. Education and Dissemination

How quality control is taught and how employees are trained through training courses and routine work in the company concerned and the related companies will be examined. To what extent the concept of quality control and statistical technologies are understood and utilized, and the activeness of QC Circle will be examined.

a. Education programs and results
b. Quality and control-consciousness, degrees of understanding of quality control
c. Teaching of statistical concepts and methods, and the extent of their dissemination
d. Grasp of the effectiveness of quality control
e. Education of related company (particularly those in the same group, subcontractors consignees, and distributors)
f. QC Circle activities
g. System of suggesting ways of improvements and its actual conditions

4. Collection, Dissemination and Use of Information

How the collection and dissemination of information on quality, from within and outside the company, are conducted by and among the head office, factories, branches, sales offices, and the organizational units will be examined, together with the evaluation of the organization and the systems used, and how fast information is transmitted, sorted, analyzed and utilized.

a. Collection of external information
b. Transmission of information between divisions
c. Speed of information transmission (use of computers)
d. Data processing, statistical analysis of information and utilization of the results

5. Analysis

Whether or not critical problems regarding quality are properly grasped and analyzed with respect to overall quality and the existing production process, and whether the results are being interpreted in the frame of the available technology will be subject to scrutiny, while a check will be made on whether proper statistical methods are being used.

a. Selection of key problems and themes
b. Propriety of the analytical approach
c. Utilization of statistical methods
d. Linkage with proper technology
e. Quality analysis, process analysis
f. Utilization of analytical results
g. Assertiveness of improvement suggestions

6. Standardization

The establishment, revision and rescission of standards and the manner of their control and systematization will be examined, together with the use of standards for the enhancement of company technology.

a. Systemization of standards
b. Method of establishing, revising, and abolishing standards
c. Outcome of the establishment, revision, or abolition of standards
d. Contents of the standards
e. Utilization of statistical methods
f. Accumulation of technology
g. Utilization of standards

7. Management System

How the procedures used for the maintenance and improvement of quality are reviewed from time to time when necessary will be examined. Also scrutinized will be how the responsibility for and the authority over these matters are defined, while a check will be made on the use of control charts and other related statistical techniques.

a. Systems for the control of quality and such related matters as cost and quality
b. Control items and control points
c. Utilization of such statistical control methods as control charts and other statistical concepts
d. Contribution to performance of QC Circle activities
e. Actual conditions of control activities
f. State of matters under control

8. Quality Assurance

New product development, quality analysis, design, production, inspection, equipment maintenance, purchasing, sales, services and other activities at each stage of the operation, which are essential for quality assurance, including reliability, will be closely examined, together with overall quality assurance management system.

a. Procedure for the development of new products and services (analysis and upgrading of quality, checking of design, reliability and other properties)
b. Safety and immunity from product liability
c. Process design, process analysis, and process control and improvement
d. Process capability
e. Instrumental, gauging, testing and inspecting
f. Equipment maintenance, and control of subcontracting, purchasing and services
g. Quality assurance system and its audit
h. Utilization of statistical methods
i. Evaluation and audit of quality
j. Actual state of quality assurance

9. Effects

What effects were produced or are being produced on the quality of products and services through the implementation of quality control will be examined? Whether products of sufficiently good quality are being manufactured and sold will be examined. Whether products have been improved from the viewpoint of quality, quantity and cost, and whether the whole company has been improved not only in the numerical effect of quality and profit, but also in the scientific way of thinking of employers and employees and their heightened will to work will be examined.

a. Measurement of effects
b. Substantive effects in quality, services, delivery time, cost, profits, safety, environment, etc.
c. Intangible effects
d. Measures for overcoming defects

10. Planning for the Future

Whether the strong and weak points in the present situation are properly recognized and whether the promotion of quality control is planned in the future and is likely to continue will be examined.

a. Grasp of the present state of affairs and the concreteness of the plan
b. Measures for overcoming defects
c. Plans for further advances
d. Linkage with the long-term plans

The Malcolm Baldrige National Quality Award shows the major areas considered important by the U.S. Department of Commerce in its administration of this award program. The categories and items have been used by companies not competing for the award as a check list for initiation of an internal quality program. Also, it can serve as a guide for individuals auditing their quality program with the objective of determining whether there are additional areas that should be addressed in the pursuit of quality.

Appendix B

Malcolm Baldrige National Quality Award
1991 Examination Categories and Items

1.0 Leadership

The Leadership category examines how senior executives create and sustain clear and visible quality values along with a management system to guide all the activities of the company toward quality excellence. Also examined are the senior executives' and the company's quality leadership in the external community and how the company integrates its public responsibilities with its quality values and practices.

1.1 Senior Executive Leadership

Describe the senior executives' leadership, personal involvement and visibility in developing and maintaining an environment for quality excellence.

AREAS TO ADDRESS

a. senior executives' leadership, personal involvement, and visibility in quality-related activities of the company: (1) goal setting; (2) planning; (3) reviewing company quality performance; (4) communicating with employees; and (5) recognizing employee contributions. Other activities may include participating in teams, learning about the quality of domestic and international competitors, and meeting with customers and suppliers.

b. senior executives' approach to building quality values into the leadership process of the company.

c. senior executives' leadership and communication of quality excellence to groups outside the company. Groups may include national, state, community, trade, business, professional, education, health care, standards and government organizations.

NOTES:

(1) The term "senior executives" refers to the highest ranking official of the organization applying for the Award and those reporting directly to that official.
(2) The type and extent of the activities of senior executives within and outside the company could depend upon company size, resources, and other business factors.

1.2 Quality Values

Describe the company's quality values, how they are projected in a consistent manner, and how adoption of the values throughout the company is determined and reinforced.

AREAS TO ADDRESS

a. a brief summary of the content of policy, mission or guidelines that demonstrate the company's quality values.

b. company's communications activities to project the quality values throughout the company. Briefly describe what is communicated and the means and frequency of communications.

c. how the company determines and evaluates how well the quality values have been adopted throughout the company, such as through surveys, interviews, or other means, and how employee adoption is reinforced.

1.3 Management for Quality

Describe how the quality values are integrated into day-to-day leadership, management, and supervision of all company units.

AREAS TO ADDRESS

a. key approaches for involving and encouraging leadership in, all levels of management and supervision in quality; principal roles and responsibilities at each level.

b. key approaches for promoting cooperation among managers and supervisors across different levels and different functions of the company.

c. types, frequency and content of reviews of company and of unit quality performance; types of actions taken to assist units not performing according to plans or goals.

d. key indicators the company uses to evaluate the effectiveness of its approaches to integrating quality values into day-to-day management and how the evaluation is used to improve its approaches.

NOTE: Key indicators refer to principal measures of some characteristics of quality or effectiveness.

1.4 Public Responsibility

Describe how the company extends its quality leadership to the external community and includes its responsibilities to the public for health, safety, environmental protection, and ethical business practice in its quality policies and improvement activities.

AREAS TO ADDRESS

a. how the company promotes quality awareness and sharing with external groups. Groups may include national, state, community, trade, business, professional, education, health care, standards and government organizations.

b. how the company encourages employee leadership and involvement in quality activities of organizations mentioned above.

c. how the company includes its public responsibilities such as business ethics, public health and safety, environmental protection, and waste management into its quality policies and practices. For each area relevant and important to the company's business, briefly summarize: (1) principal quality improvement goals and how they are set; (2) principal improvement methods; (3) principal indicators used to monitor quality; and (4) how and how often progress is reviewed.

NOTE: Health and safety of employees are not covered in this item. These are addressed in Item 4.5.

2.0 Information and Analysis

The Information and Analysis category examines the scope, validity, use, and management of data and information that underlie the company's overall quality management system. Also examined is the adequacy of the data, information, and analysis to support a responsive, prevention-based approach to quality and customer satisfaction built upon "management by fact."

2.1 Scope and Management of Quality Data and Information

Describe the company's base of data and information used for planning, day-to-day management, and evaluation of quality, and how data and information reliability, timeliness, and access are assured.

AREAS TO ADDRESS

a. (1) criteria for selecting data to be included in the quality-related data and information base; and (2) scope and types of data: customer-related; internal operations and processes; employee-related; safety, health and regulatory; quality performance; supplier quality; and other.

b. processes and techniques the company uses to ensure reliability, consistency, standardization, review, timely update, and rapid access throughout the company. If applicable, describe approach to ensuring software quality.

c. how the company evaluates and improves the scope and quality of its data and information and how it shortens the cycle from data gathering to access.

NOTES:

(1) The purpose of this item is to permit the applicant to demonstrate the breadth and depth of the data assembled as part of its total quality management system. Applicants should give brief descriptions of the types of data under major headings such as "employees" and subheadings such as "education and training," "teams," and "recognition." Under each subheading, give a brief description of the data and information. Actual data should not be reported in this item. Such data are requested in other Examination items.

(2) Information on the scope and management of competitive and benchmark data is requested in Item 2.2.

2.2 Competitive Comparisons and Benchmarks

Describe the company's approach to selecting quality-related competitive comparisons and world-class benchmarks to support quality planning, evaluation, and improvement.

AREAS TO ADDRESS

a. criteria and rationale the company uses for seeking competitive comparisons and benchmarks: (1) relationship to company goals and priorities for improvement of product and service quality and/or company operations; (2) with whom to compare—within and outside the company's industry.

b. current scope of competitive and benchmark data: (1) product and service quality; (2) customer satisfaction and other customer data; (3) supplier performance; (4) employee data; (5) internal operations, business processes, and support services; and (6) other. For each type: (a) list sources of comparisons and benchmarks, including company and independent testing or evaluation; and (b) how each type of data is used.

c. how the company evaluates and improves the scope, sources, and uses of competitive and benchmark data.

NOTE:This item focuses primarily on analysis for company-level evaluation and decision making. Some other items request information based on analysis of specific sets of data for special purposes such as human resource practices and complaint management.

2.3 Analysis of Quality Data and Information

Describe how data and information are analyzed to support the company's overall quality objectives.

AREAS TO ADDRESS

a. how data described in 2.1 and 2.2, separately and in combination, are analyzed to support: (1) company planning and priorities; (2) company-level review of quality performance; (3) improvement of internal operations, business processes, and support services; (4) determination of product and service features and levels of quality performance that best predict improvement in customer satisfaction; and (5) quality improvement projections based upon potential use of alternative strategies or technologies.

b. how the company evaluates and improves its analytical capabilities and shortens the cycle of analysis and access to analytical results.

3.0 Strategic Quality Planning

The Strategic Quality Planning category examines the company's planning process for achieving or retaining quality leadership and how the company integrates quality improvement planning into overall business planning. Also examined are the company's short-term and longer-term plans to achieve and/or sustain a quality leadership position.

3.1 Strategic Quality Planning Process

Describe the company's strategic quality planning process for short-term (1-2 years) and longer-term (3 years or more) quality leadership and customer satisfaction.

AREAS TO ADDRESS

a. how goals for quality leadership are set using: (1) current and future quality requirements for leadership in the company's target markets; and (2) company's current quality levels and trends versus competitors' in these markets.

b. principal types of data, information, and analysis used in developing plans and evaluating feasibility based upon goals: (1) customer requirements; (2) process capabilities; (3) competitive and benchmark data; and (4) supplier capabilities; outline how these data are used in developing plans.

c. how strategic plans and goals are implemented and reviewed: (1) how specific plans, goals, and performance indicators are deployed to all work units and suppliers; (2) how resources are committed for key requirements such as capital expenditures and training; and (3) how performance relative to plans and goals is reviewed and acted upon.

d. how the goal-setting and strategic planning processes are evaluated and improved.

NOTES:

(1) Strategic quality plans address in detail how the company will pursue market leadership through providing superior quality products and services and through improving the effectiveness of all operations of the company.

(2) Item 3.1 focuses on the processes of goal setting and strategic planning. Item 3.2 focuses on actual goals and plans.

3.2 Quality Goals and Plans

Summarize the company's goals and strategies. Outline principal quality plans for the short-term (1-2 years) and longer-term (3 years or more).

AREAS TO ADDRESS

a. major quality goals and principal strategies for achieving these goals.

b. principal short-term plans: (1) summary of key requirements and performance indicators deployed to work units and suppliers; and (2) resources committed to accomplish the key requirements.

c. principal longer-term plans: brief summary of major requirements, and how they will be met.

d. two-to-five-year projection of significant changes in the company's most important quality levels. Describe how these levels may be expected to compare with those of key competitors over this time period.

NOTE:

The company's most important quality levels are those for the key product and service quality features. Projections are estimates of future quality levels based upon implementation of the plans described in Item 3.2.

4.0 Human Resource Utilization

The Human Resource Utilization category examines the effectiveness of the company's efforts to develop and realize the full potential of the work force, including management, and to maintain an environment conducive to full participation, quality leadership, and personal and organizational growth.

4.1 Human Resource Management

Describe how the company's overall human resource management effort supports its quality objectives.

AREAS TO ADDRESS

a. how human resource plans are derived from the quality goals, strategies, and plans outlined in 3.2: (1) short-term (1-2 years); and (2) longer-term (3 years or more). Address major specific requirements such as training, development, hiring, involvement, empowerment, and recognition.
b. key quality goals and improvement methods for human resource management practices such as hiring and career development.
c. how the company analyzes and uses its overall employee-related data to evaluate and improve the effectiveness of all categories and all types of employees.

NOTES:
(1) Human resource plans and improvement activities might include one or more of the following: mechanisms for promoting cooperation such as internal customer/supplier techniques or other internal partnerships; initiatives to promote labor-management cooperation such as partnerships with unions; creation or modifications in recognition systems; mechanisms for increasing or broadening employee responsibilities; and education and training initiatives. They might also include developing partnerships with educational institutions to develop employees and to help ensure the future supply of well-prepared employees.
(2) "Types of employees" takes into account factors such as employment status, bargaining unit membership, and demographic makeup.

4.2 Employee Involvement

Describe the means available for all employees to contribute effectively to meeting the company's quality objectives; summarize trends and current levels of involvement.

AREAS TO ADDRESS

a. management practices and specific mechanisms, such as teams or suggestion systems, the company uses to promote employee contributions to quality objectives, individually and in groups. Summarize how and when the company gives feedback.
b. company actions to increase employee authority to act (empowerment), responsibility, and innovation. Summarize principal goals for all categories of employees.
c. key indicators the company uses to evaluate the extent and effectiveness of involvement by all categories and types of employees and how the indicators are used to improve employee involvement.
d. trends and current levels of involvement by all categories of employees. Use the most important indicator(s) of effective employee involvement for each category of employees.

NOTE: Different involvement goals and indicators may be set for different categories of employees, depending upon company needs and upon the types of responsibilities of each employee category.

4.3 Quality Education and Training

Describe how the company decides what quality education and training is needed by employees and how it utilizes the knowledge and skills acquired; summarize the types of quality education and training received by employees in all employee categories.

AREAS TO ADDRESS

a. (1) how the company assesses needs for the types and amounts of quality education and training received by all categories of employees (describe how the needs assessment addresses work unit requirements to include or have access to skills in problem analysis and problem solving to meet their quality objectives); (2) methods for the delivery of quality education and training; and (3) how the company ensures on-the-job reinforcement of knowledge and skills.

b. summary and trends in quality education and training received by employees. The summary and trends should address: (1) quality orientation of new employees; (2) percent of employees receiving quality education and training in each employee category annually; (3) average hours of quality education and training annually per employee; (4) percent of employees who have received quality education and training; and (5) percent of employees who have received education and training in statistical and other quantitative problem-solving methods.

c. key methods and indicators the company uses to evaluate and improve the effectiveness of its quality education and training. Describe how the indicators are used to improve the quality education and training of all categories and types of employees.

NOTE: Quality education and training addresses the knowledge and skills employees need to meet the quality objectives associated with their responsibilities. This may include basic quality awareness, problem solving, meeting customer requirement, and other quality-related aspects of skills.

4.4 Employee Recognition and Performance Measurement

Describe how the company's recognition and performance measurement processes support quality objectives; summarize trends in recognition.

AREAS TO ADDRESS

a. how recognition, reward, and performance measurement for individuals and groups, including managers, support the company's quality objectives; (1) how quality relative to other business considerations such as schedules and financial results is reinforced; and (2) how employees are involved in the development and improvement of performance measurements.

b. trends in recognition and reward of individuals and groups, by employee category, for contributions to quality.

c. key indicators the company uses to evaluate and improve its recognition, reward, and performance measurement processes.

4.5 Employee Well-Being and Morale

Describe how the company maintains a work environment conducive to the well-being and growth of all employees; summarize trends and levels in key indicators of well-being and morale.

AREAS TO ADDRESS

a. how well-being and morale factors such as health, safety, satisfaction, and ergonomics are included in quality improvement activities. Summarize principal improvement goals and methods for each factor relevant and important to the company's work environment. For accidents and work-related health problems, describe how underlying causes are determined and how adverse conditions are prevented.

b. mobility, flexibility, and retraining in job assignments to support employee development and/or to accommodate changes in technology, improved productivity, or changes in work processes.

c. special services, facilities and opportunities the company makes available to employees. These might include one or more of the following: counseling, assistance, recreational or cultural, and non-work-related education.

d. how employee satisfaction is determined and interpreted for use in quality improvement.

e. trends and levels in key indicators of well-being and morale such as safety, absenteeism, turnover, attrition rate for customer-contact personnel, satisfaction, grievances, strikes, and worker compensation. Explain important adverse results, if any, and how problems were resolved or current status. Compare the current levels of the most significant indicators with those of industry averages and industry leaders.

5.0 Quality Assurance of Products and Services

The Quality Assurance of Products and Services category examines the systematic approaches used by the company for assuring quality of goods and services based primarily upon process design and control, including control of procured materials, parts, and services. Also examined is the integration of process control with continuous quality improvement.

5.1 Design and Introduction of Quality Products and Services

Describe how new and/or improved products and services are designed and introduced and how processes are designed to meet key product and service quality requirements.

AREAS TO ADDRESS

a. how designs of products, services, and processes are developed so that: (1) customer requirements are translated into design requirements; (2) all quality requirements are addressed early in the overall design process by all appropriate company units; (3) designs are coordinated and integrated to include all phases of production and delivery; and (4) a process control plan is developed that involves selecting and setting key process characteristics for production and delivery of products and services and how these characteristics are to be measured and controlled.

b. how designs are reviewed and validated taking into account key factors: (1) product and service performance; (2) process capability and future requirements; and (3) supplier capability and future requirements.

c. how the company evaluates and improves the effectiveness of its designs and design processes and how it shortens the design-to-introduction cycle.

NOTES:

(1) Design and introduction may include modification and variants of existing products and services and/or new products and services emerging from research and development.

(2) Service and manufacturing businesses should interpret product and service requirements to include all product-and-service requirements at all stages of production, delivery, and use. See also Item 7.1, Note (3).

(3) Depending on their type of business, applicants need to consider many factors in product and service design such as health, safety, long-term performance, measurement capability, process capability, maintainability, and supplier capability. Applicant responses should reflect the key requirements of the products and services they deliver.

5.2 Process Quality Control

Describe how the processes used to produce the company's products and services are controlled.

AREAS TO ADDRESS

a. how the company assures that processes are controlled within limits set in process design. Include information on: (1) types and frequencies of measurements; and (2) what is measured, such as process, product, and service characteristics.

b. for out-of-control occurrences, describe: (1) how root causes are determined; (2) how corrections are made so that future occurrences are prevented; and (3) how corrections are verified.

c. how the company evaluates the quality of the measurements used in process

---

NOTES:

(1) For manufacturing and service companies with measurement requirements, it is necessary to demonstrate that measurement accuracy and precision meet process, service, and product requirements (measurement quality assurance). For physical, chemical and engineering measurements, indicate approaches for ensuring that measurements are traceable to national standards through calibrations, reference materials or other means.

(2) Verification of corrections and verification of improvements in 5.2b, 5.3c, and 5.4b should include comparison with expected or predicted results.

5.3 Continuous Improvement of Processes

Describe how processes used to produce products and services are continuously improved.

AREAS TO ADDRESS

a. principal types of data and information the company uses to determine needs and opportunities for improvement in processes: (1) data from day-to-day process control; (2) field data such as customer data, data on product and service performance, and data on competitors' performance; (3) evaluation of all process steps; (4) process benchmark data; and (5) data of other types such as from process research and development and evaluation of new technology or alternative processes.

b. how the company evaluates potential changes in processes to select from among alternatives.

c. how the company integrates process improvement with day-to-day process quality control; (1) resetting process characteristics; (2) verification

---

NOTE: The focus of this item is on improvement of the primary processes used to produce the company's products and services, not on maintaining them or on correcting out-of-control occurrences, which is the focus of item 5.2.

5.4 Quality Assessment

Describe how the company assesses the quality of its systems, processes, practices, products, and services.

AREAS TO ADDRESS

a. approaches the company uses to assess the quality of its systems, processes, practices, products, and services such as process reviews or audits. Include the types and frequencies of assessments, what is assessed, who conducts the assessments, and how the validity of assessment tools is assured.

b. how assessment findings are used to improve systems, processes, practices, training, or supplier requirements. Include how the company

---

5.5 Documentation

Describe documentation and other modes of knowledge preservation and knowledge transfer to support quality assurance, quality assessment, and quality improvement.

AREAS TO ADDRESS

a. (1) principal quality-related purposes of documents such as for recording procedures and practices and for retaining key records; and (2) uses of documents such as in standardization, orientation of new employees, training, maintaining records for legal purposes, or for quality-related tracking of products, processes, and services.

b. how the company improves its documentation system: (1) to simplify and harmonize documents; (2) to keep pace with changes in practice, technology, and systems; (3) to ensure rapid access wherever needed; and (4) to dispose of obsolete documents.

NOTE: Documents may be written or computerized.

5.6 Business Process and Support Service Quality

Summarize process quality, quality assessment, and quality improvement activities for business processes and support services.

AREAS TO ADDRESS

a. summary of process quality control and quality assessment activities for key business processes and support services: (1) how principal process quality requirements are set using customer requirements or the requirements of other company units served ("internal customers"); (2) how and how often process quality is measured; and (3) types and frequencies of quality assessments and who conducts them.

b. summary of quality improvement activities for key business processes and support services: (1) principal quality improvement goals and how they are set; (2) principal process evaluation and improvement activities, including how processes are simplified and response time shortened; (3) principal indicators used to measure quality; and (4) how and how often progress is reviewed.

NOTES:

(1) Business processes and support services might include activities and operations involving finance and accounting, software services, sales, marketing, information services, purchasing, personnel, legal services, plant and facilities management, research and development, and secretarial and other administrative services.

(2) The purpose of this item is to permit applicants to highlight separately the quality assurance, quality assessment, and quality improvement activities for functions that support the primary processes through which products and services are produced and delivered. Together, Items 5.1, 5.2, 5.3, 5.4, 5.5, 5.6 and 5.7 should cover all operations, processes, and activities of all work units. However, the selection of support services and business processes for inclusion in Item 5.6 depends on the type of business and quality system and should be made by the applicant.

5.7 Supplier Quality

Describe how the quality of materials, components, and services furnished by other businesses is assured, assessed and improved.

AREAS TO ADDRESS

a. approaches used to define and communicate the company's specific quality requirements to suppliers. Include: (1) the principal quality requirements for the company's most important suppliers; and (2) the principal quality indicators the company uses to communicate and monitor supplier quality.

b. methods used to assure that the company's quality requirements are met by suppliers. Methods may include audits, process reviews, receiving inspection, certification, and testing.

c. strategy and current actions to improve the quality and responsiveness of suppliers. These may include partnerships, training, incentives and recognition, and supplier selection.

NOTE: The term "supplier" as used here refers to other company providers of goods and services. The use of these goods and services may occur at any stage in the production, delivery, and use of the company's products and services. Thus, suppliers include businesses such as distributors, dealers, and franchises as well as those that provide materials and components.

6.0 Quality Results

The Quality Results category examines quality levels and quality improvement based upon objective measures derived from analysis of customer requirements and expectations and from analysis of business operations. Also examined are current quality levels in relation to those of competing firms.

6.1 Product and Service Quality Results

Summarize trends in quality improvement and current quality levels for key product and service features; compare the company's current quality levels with those of competitors and world leaders.

AREAS TO ADDRESS

a. trends and current levels for all key measures of product and service quality.

b. current quality level comparisons with principal competitors in the company's key markets, industry averages, industry leaders, and world leaders. Briefly explain bases for comparison such as: (1) independent surveys, studies, or laboratory testing; (2) benchmarks; and (3) company evaluations and testing. Describe how objectivity and validity of comparisons are assured.

NOTES:

(1) Key product and service measures are measures relative to the set of all important features of the company's products and services. These measures, taken together, best represent the most important factors that predict customer satisfaction and quality in customer use. Examples include measures of accuracy, reliability, timeliness, performance, behavior, delivery, after-sales services, documentation, and appearance. These measures are "internal" measures. Customer satisfaction or other customer data should not be included in response to this item.

(2) Results reported in Item 6.1 should reflect the key product and service features determined in Item 7.1, and be fully consistent with the key quality requirements for products and services described in the Overview.

6.2 Business Process, Operational, and Support Service Quality Results

Summarize trends in quality improvement and current quality levels for business processes, operations, and support services.

AREAS TO ADDRESS

a. trends and current levels for the most important measures of the quality and effectiveness of business processes, operations, and support services.

b. comparison with industry averages, industry leaders, and world leaders.

NOTES:

(1) Key measures for business processes, operations, and support services are the set of principal measurable characteristics that represent quality and effectiveness in company operations in meeting requirements of customers and of other company units. Examples include measures of accuracy, timeliness, and effectiveness. Measures include error rates, defect rates, lead times, cycle times, and use of manpower, materials, energy, and capital as reflected in indicators such as repeat services, utilization rates, and waste.

(2) The results reported in Item 6.2 derive from quality improvement activities described in Category 5 and Item 1.4, if appropriate. Responses should reflect relevance to the company's principal quality objectives and should also demonstrate the breadth of improvement results throughout all operations and work units.

6.3 Supplier Quality Results

Summarize trends and levels in quality of suppliers and services furnished by other companies, compare the company's supplier quality with that of competitors and with key benchmarks.

AREAS TO ADDRESS

a. trends and current levels for the most important indicators of supplier quality.

b. comparison of the company's supplier quality with that of competitors and/or with benchmarks. Such comparisons could include industry averages, industry leaders, world leaders, principal competitors in the company's key markets, and appropriate benchmarks. Describe the

---

NOTE: The results reported in Item 6.3 derive from quality improvement activities described in Item 5.7. Results should be broken down by major groupings of suppliers and reported using the principal quality indicators described in Item 5.7.

7.0 Customer Satisfaction

The Customer Satisfaction category examines the company's knowledge of the customer, overall customer service systems, responsiveness, and its ability to meet requirements and expectations. Also examined are current levels and trends in customer satisfaction.

7.1 Determining Customer Requirements and Expectations

Describe how the company determines current and future customer requirements and expectations.

AREAS TO ADDRESS

a. how the company determines current and future requirements and expectations of customers. Include information on: (1) how market segments and customer groups are determined and how customers of competitors and other potential customers are considered; (2) the process for collecting information and data. This should include what information is sought, frequencies of surveys, interviews or other contacts, and how objectivity is assured; (3) how other information and data are cross-compared to support determination of customer requirements and expectations. Such information and data might include performance information on the company's products and services, complaints, gains and losses of customers, customer satisfaction, and competitors' performance.

b. process for determining product and service features and the relative importance of these features to customers and/or customer groups

c. how the company evaluates and improves its processes for determining customer requirements and expectations as well as the key product and service features

---

NOTES:

(1) Products and services may be sold to end users by intermediaries such as retail stores or dealers. Thus, determining customer groups should take into account both the end users and the intermediaries.

(2) Product and service features refer to all important characteristics of products and services experienced by the customers throughout the overall purchase and ownership experiences. This includes any factors that bear upon customer preference or customer view of quality—for example, those features that enhance them or differentiate them from competing offerings.

(3) An applicant may choose to describe its offerings, part of its offerings, or certain of its activities as products or services irrespective of the SIC classification of the company. Such descriptions should then be consistent throughout the Application Report.

7.2 Customer Relationship Management

Describe how the company provides effective management of its relationships with its customers and uses information gained from customers to improve products and services as well as its customer relationship management practices.

AREAS TO ADDRESS

a. means for ensuring easy access for customers to seek assistance and to comment. Describe types of contact, such as telephone, personal, and written, and how the company maintains easy access for each type of contact.

b. follow-up with customers on products and services to determine satisfaction with recent transactions and to seek data and information for improvement.

c. how the following are addressed for customer-contact personnel: (1) selection factors for customer-contact jobs; (2) career path; (3) special training to include: knowledge of products and services, listening to customers, soliciting comment from customers, how to anticipate and handle special problems or failures, and skills in customer retention; (4) empowerment and decision making; (5) attitude and morale determination; (6) recognition and reward; and (7) attrition.

d. how the company provides technical and logistics support for customer-contact personnel to enable them to provide reliable and responsive services.

e. how the company analyzes key customer-related data and information to assess costs and market consequences for policy development, planning, and resource allocation.

f. principal factors the company uses to evaluate its customer relationship management, such as response accuracy, timeliness, and customer satisfaction with contacts. Describe how the factors or indicators are used to improve training, technology, or customer-oriented management practices.

NOTES:
(1) Other key aspects of customer relationship management are addressed in Items 7.3, 7.4, and 7.5.
(2) Item 7.2c addresses important human resource management requirements specifically for customer-contact personnel. This is included in Item 7.2 for special emphasis and coherence.

7.3 Customer Service Standards

Describe the company's standards governing the direct contact between its employees and customers, and how these standards are set and modified.

AREAS TO ADDRESS

a. how well-defined service standards to meet customer requirements are set. List and briefly describe the company's most important customer service standards.

b. how standards requirements and key standards information are deployed to company units that support customer-contact personnel. Briefly describe how the company ensures that the support provided by these company units is effective and timely.

c. how service standards are tracked, evaluated, and improved. Describe the role of customer-contact personnel in evaluating and improving standards.

NOTE: Service standards are objectively measurable levels of performance that define quality for the overall service or for a part of a service. Examples include measures of response time, problem resolution time, accuracy, and completeness.

7.4 Commitment to Customers

Describe the company's commitments to customers on its explicit and implicit promises underlying its products and services.

AREAS TO ADDRESS

a. types of commitments the company makes to promote trust and confidence in its products, services, and relationships. Include how the company ensures that these commitments: (1) address the principal concerns of customers; (2) are free from conditions that might weaken customer confidence; and (3) are understandable.

b. how improvements in the quality of the company's products and services over the past three years have been translated into stronger commitments. Compare commitments with those of competing companies.

NOTE: Commitments may include product and service guarantees, product warranties, and other understandings with the customer, expressed or implied.

7.5 Complaint Resolution for Quality Improvement

Describe how the company handles complaints, resolves them, and uses complaint information for quality improvement and for prevention of recurrence of problems.

AREAS TO ADDRESS

a. how the company ensures that formal and informal complaints and feedback given to different company units are aggregated for overall evaluation and use wherever appropriate throughout the company.

b. how the company ensures that complaints are resolved promptly and effectively. Include: (1) trends and levels in indicators of response time; and (2) trends in percent of complaints resolved on first contact with customer-contact personnel.

c. how complaints are analyzed to determine underlying causes and how the findings are translated into improvements. This translation may lead to improvements such as in processes, service standards, training of customer-contact personnel, and information to customers to help them make more effective use of products and/or services.

d. key indicators and methods the company uses to evaluate and improve its complaint-related processes. Describe how indicators and methods address effectiveness, response time improvement, and translation of findings into improvements.

NOTES:
(1) A major purpose of aggregation of complaint information is to ensure overall evaluation for policy development, planning, training, and resource allocation. However, this does not imply that complaint resolution and quality improvement should await aggregation or that resolution and improvement are necessarily centralized within a company.
(2) Trends and current levels in complaints are requested in Item 7.7.

7.6 Determining Customer Satisfaction

Describe the company's methods for determining customer satisfaction, how satisfaction information is used in quality improvement, and how methods for determining customer satisfaction are improved.

AREAS TO ADDRESS

a. how the company determines customer satisfaction for customer groups. Address: (1) brief description of market segments and customer groups; and (2) the process for determining customer satisfaction for customer groups. Include what information is sought, frequency of surveys, interviews or other contacts, and how objectivity is assured. Describe how the company sets the customer satisfaction measurement scale to adequately capture key information that accurately reflects customer preference.

b. how customer satisfaction relative to competitors is determined.

c. how customer satisfaction data are analyzed and compared with other customer satisfaction indicators such as complaints and gains and losses of customers. Describe how such comparisons are used to improve customer satisfaction determination.

d. how the company evaluates and improves its overall methods and measurement scales used in determining customer satisfaction and customer satisfaction relative to competitors.

NOTES:

(1) Information sought in determining customer satisfaction may include specific product and service features and the relative importance of these features to customers, thus supplementing information sought in determining customer requirements and expectations.

(2) The customer satisfaction measurement scale may include both numerical designators and the descriptors assigned to them. An effective scale is one that provides the company with accurate information about specific product and service features and about the customers' likely market behaviors.

7.7 Customer Satisfaction Results

Summarize trends in the company's customer satisfaction and in indicators of adverse customer response.

AREAS TO ADDRESS

a. trends in current levels in indicators of customer satisfaction for products and services. Segment these results by customer groups, as appropriate.

b. trends and current levels in major adverse indicators. Adverse indicators include complaints, claims, refunds, recalls, returns, repeat services, litigation, replacements, downgrades, repairs, warranty costs, and warranty work. If the company has received any sanctions under regulation or contract over the past three years, include such information in this item. Briefly describe how sanctions were resolved or current status.

7.8 Customer Satisfaction Comparison

Compare the company's customer satisfaction results and recognition with those of competitors that provide similar products and services.

AREAS TO ADDRESS

a. comparison of customer satisfaction results. Such comparisons should be made with principal competitors in the company's key markets, industry averages, industry leaders, and world leaders.

b. surveys, competitive awards, recognition and ratings by independent organizations, including customers. Briefly describe surveys, awards, recognition, and ratings. Include how quality and quality attributes are considered as factors in the evaluations of these independent organizations.

c. trends in gaining or losing customers and in customer and customer account retention. Briefly summarize gains and losses of customers, including those gained from or lost to competitors. Address customer groups or market segments, as appropriate.

d. trends in gaining and losing market share relative to major competitors,

The terms and definitions for quality have been collected and recorded from a variety of sources. The collection of these terms and definitions includes more than one definition for the same term because the author is not recommending one definition over another, and the reader has the choice of using any or all of the definitions. The asterisk (*) denotes the terms and related definitions used in this book.

Appendix C

Terms and Definitions

This Appendix provides terms and definitions pertaining to quality management. These terms are recognized as the ones most commonly accepted and used within the field of quality.

The sources of the terms and definitions are shown to permit traceability to the original document in case of conflicting definitions. The abbreviations in the sources are: CII - Construction Industry Institute; DODD - Department of Defense Directive; Federal Acquisition Regulation - FAR; ISO - International Standards Organization; MIL-HDBK - military handbook; MIL-STD - military standard; MIL-(x) - Military Specification ("x" implying the first character of the title, e.g., "Q" for Quality); and PMBOK - Project Management Body of Knowledge.

Acceptability Criteria. A limit or limits placed upon the degree of nonconformance permitted in material expressed in definitive operational terms. (Source: MIL-STD 109A)

Acceptable Quality Level (AQL). The maximum percent defective (or the maximum number of defects per hundred units) that, for the purpose of sampling inspection, can be considered satisfactory as a process average. (Source: MIL-STD 105)

*Acceptance. The act of an authorized representative of the government by which the government, for itself or as agent for another, assumes ownership of existing identified supplies tendered or approves specific services rendered as partial or complete performance of the contract. (Source: FAR 46.101)

Acceptance Number. The maximum number of defects or defective units in the sample that will permit acceptance of the inspection lot or batch. (Source: MIL-STD 109A)

Analysis. The study and examination of something complex and separation into its more simple components. Analysis typically includes discovering not only what are the parts of the thing being studied, but also how they fit together and why they are arranged in this particular way. A study of schedule variances for cause, impact, and corrective action. (Source: PMBOK)

*Attribute. A characteristic or property which is appraised in terms of whether it does or does not exist, (e.g., go or not-go) with respect to a given requirement. (Source: MIL-HDBK H53)

*Audit. A planned and documented activity performed by qualified personnel to determine by investigation, examination, or evaluation of objective evidence, the adequacy and compliance with established procedures, or applicable documents, and the effectiveness of implementation. (Source: PMBOK)

Average Outgoing Quality (AOQ). The average quality of outgoing product including all accepted lots, plus all rejected lots after the rejected lots have been effectively 100 percent inspected and all defectives replaced by non-defectives. (Source: MIL-STD 105)

Average Outgoing Quality Limit (AOQL). The maximum of the average outgoing qualities for all possible incoming qualities for a given sampling plan. (Source: MIL-STD 105)

Average Sample Size Curve. The curves that show the average sample sizes which may be expected to occur under the various sampling plans for a given process quality. (Source: MIL-STD 105)

Batch. See "Lot."

*Bulk Material. Material bought in lots; generally, no specific item is distinguishable from any other in the lot. These items can be purchased from a standard catalog description and are bought in quantity for distribution as required. (Source: PMBOK)

*Calibration. Comparison of two instruments or measuring devices, one of which is a standard of known accuracy traceable to national standards, to detect, correlate, report, or eliminate by adjustment any discrepancy in accuracy or the instrument or measuring device being compared with the standard. (Source: MIL- C-45662)

Certificate of Conformance. A contractor's written statement, when authorized by contract, certifying that supplies or services comply with contract requirements. (Source: FAR 46.315)

*Characteristic. A physical, chemical, visual, functional or any other identifiable property of a product of material. (Source: MIL-STD 109A)

Classification of Defects. The enumeration of possible defects of the unit of product, classified according to their seriousness. Defects will normally be grouped into the classes of critical, major or minor; however, they may be grouped into other classes, or into subclasses within these classes. (Source: MIL- STD 105)

Clearance Number (i). Is the number of successively inspected units which must be found free of defects concerned before a certain action to change the inspection procedure can be taken. (Source: MIL-HDBK H107)

Client Quality Services. The process of creating a two-way feedback system to define expectations, opportunities, and anticipated needs. (Source: PMBOK)

*Company. Term used primarily to refer to a business first party, the purpose of which is to supply a product or service. (Source: ISO 9004)

*Concession; Waiver. Written authorization to use or release a quantity of material, components or stores already produced but which do not conform to the specified requirements. (Source: ISO 8402)

*Contract Quality Requirements. The technical requirements in the contract relating to the quality of the product or service and those contract clauses prescribing inspection, and other quality controls incumbent on the contractor, to assure that the product or service conforms to the contractual requirements. (Source: FAR 46.101)

Cost of Quality. The total price of all efforts to achieve product or service quality. This includes all work to build a product or service that conforms to the requirements as well as all work that results from nonconformance to the requirements. The cost of quality is divided into internal—those costs associated with building the product or service—and external—the costs associated with the product or service after it leaves the originating activity or company. (Source: PMBOK)

*Cost of Quality. Those costs associated with: (1) quality management activities (prevention and appraisal); and (2) those costs associated with correcting deviations. It does not include the normal costs of performing the work. (Source: CII Publication 10-2)

*Correction. The elimination of a defect. (Source: FAR 46.701)

Critical Defect. A defect that judgment and experience indicate is likely to result in hazardous or unsafe conditions for individuals using, maintaining, or depending upon the product; or a defect that judgment and experience indicate is likely to prevent performance of the tactical function of a major end item such as an aircraft, communication system, land vehicle, missile, ship, space vehicle, surveillance system, or major part thereof. (Source: MIL-STD 105)

Critical Defective. A unit of product that contains one or more critical defects and may also contain major or minor defects. (Source: MIL-STD 105)

*Customer. Ultimate consumer, user, client, beneficiary or second party. (Source: ISO 9004)

*Defect. Any nonconformance of a characteristic with specified requirements. (Source: MIL-STD 105)

Defect. The nonfulfillment of intended usage requirements. (Source: ISO 8402)

*Defective. A unit of product which contains one or more defects. (Source: MIL-STD 105)

Defects-Per-Hundred-Units. The number of defects-per-hundred units of any given quality of product is the number of defects contained therein divided by the total number of units of product, the quotient multiplied by one hundred (one or more defects being possible in any unit of product). Expressed as an equation: Defects per hundred units = Number of Defects x 100 divided by Number of Units. (Source: MIL-STD 105)

Design of Experiment. The planning of an experiment to minimize the cost of data obtained and maximize the validity of range of results. Each experiment contains three parts: the experimental statement, the design, and the analysis. (Source: PMBOK)

*Design Review. A formal, documented, comprehensive and systematic examination of a design to evaluate the design requirements and the capability of the design to meet these requirements and to identify problems and propose solutions. (Source: ISO 8402)

Deviation. Written authorization, granted prior to the manufacture of an item, to depart from a particular performance or design requirement of a contract, specification, or referenced document, for a specific number of units or specific period of time. (Source: DODD 5010.19)

*Deviation. A departure from established requirements. Deviations occur when the work product either fails to meet or unnecessarily exceeds the requirements. (Source: CII Publication 10-2)

*Examination. An element of inspection consisting of investigation, without the use of special laboratory appliances or procedures, of supplies and services to determine conformance to those specified requirements which can be determined by such investigations. Examination is generally non-destructive and includes, but is not limited to visual, auditory, olfactory, tactile, gustatory, and other investigations; simple physical manipulation; gauging, and measurement. (Source: MIL-STD 109A)

Formative Quality Evaluation. The process of reviewing the project data at key junctures during the project's life cycle for a comparative analysis against the pre-established quality specifications. This evaluation is ongoing during the life of the project to ensure that timely changes can be made as needed to protect the success of the project. (Source: PMBOK)

Function Quality Integration. The process of actively ensuring that quality plans and programs are integrated, mutually consistent, necessary and sufficient to permit the project team to achieve the defined product quality. (Source: PMBOK)

Government Contract Quality Assurance. The various functions, including inspection, performed by the government to determine whether a contractor has fulfilled the contract obligations pertaining to quality and quantity. (Source: FAR 46.101)

*Grade.

An indicator of category or rank related to features or characteristics that cover different sets of needs for products or services intended for the same functional use. (Source: ISO 8402)

Inspection. Examining and testing supplies of services (including, when appropriate, raw materials, components, and intermediate assemblies) to determine whether they conform to contract requirements. (Source: FAR 46.101)

*Inspection. Activities such as measuring, examining, testing, gauging one or more characteristics of a product or service and comparing these with specified requirements to determine conformity. (Source: ISO 8402)

*Inspection by Attributes. Inspection whereby either the unit of product or characteristics thereof, is classified simply as defective or nondefective, or the number of defects in the unit of product is counted, with respect to a given requirement. (Source: MIL-STD 105)

Inspection by Variables. Inspection wherein certain quality characteristics of sample are evaluated with respect to a continuous numerical scale and expressed as precise points along this scale. Variables inspection records the degree of conformance or nonconformance of the unit with specified requirements for the quality characteristics involved. (Source: MIL-STD 105)

Inspection Cyclical. A system whereby supplies and equipment in storage are subjected to, but not limited to, periodic, and special inspection and continuous action to assure that material is maintained in a ready for issue condition. (Source: MIL-STD 105)

Inspection In-Process. Inspection which is performed during the manufacturing or repair cycle in an effort to prevent defectives from occurring and to inspect the characteristics and attributes which are not capable of being inspected at final inspection. (Source: MIL-STD 105)

Inspection Level. An indication of the relative sample size for a given amount of product. (Source: MIL-STD 105)

Inspection, Original. First inspection of a particular quantity of product as distinguished from the inspection of product which has been resubmitted after prior rejection. (Source: MIL-STD 105)

*Inspection, Quality Conformance. All examinations and tests performed on items or services for the purpose of determining conformance with specified requirements. (Source: Defense Standardization Manual 4120.3-M)

*Inspection Record. Recorded data concerning the results of inspection action. (Source: MIL-STD 105)

Inspection System Requirement. A requirement to establish and maintain an inspection system in accordance with government specification, MIL-I-45208. The requirement is referenced in contracts when technical requirements are such as to require control of quality by in-process as well as final, end item inspection. (Source: FAR)

Inspection Tightened. Inspection under a sampling plan using the same quality level as for normal inspection, but requiring more stringent acceptance criteria. (Source: MIL-STD 109A)

Limiting Quality (LQ). The maximum defective in product quality (or the worst product quality) that the consumer is willing to accept at a specified probability of occurrence. (Source: MIL-HDBK H53)

*Lot. A collection of units of product bearing identification and treated as a unique entity from which a sample is to be drawn and inspected to determine conformance with the acceptability criteria. (Source: MIL-STD 105)

Lot Formation. The procedure of collecting, segregating, or delineating production units into homogeneous identifiable groups according to type, grade, class, size, composition, or condition of manufacture. (Source: MIL-STD 109A)

*Lot Size. The number of units of product in a lot. (Source: MIL-STD 105)

*Maintainability. A characteristic of design and installation which is expressed as the probability that restored to a specified condition within a given period of time, when the maintenance is performed in accordance with prescribed procedures and resources. (Source: MIL-STD 721)

Maintenance Quality Assurance. The determination that material maintained, overhauled, rebuilt, modified, and reclaimed conforms to the prescribed technical requirements. (Source: DODD 4155.15)

Major Defect. A defect other than critical, that is likely to result in failure, or to reduce materially the usability of the unit of product for its intended purpose. (Source: MIL-STD 105)

Major Defective. A unit of product that contains one or more major defects, and may also contain minor defects but contains no critical defect. (Source: MIL-STD 105)

Managerial Quality Administration. The managerial process of defining and monitoring policies, responsibilities and systems necessary to retain quality standards throughout the project. (Source: PMBOK)

Material Review Board. The formal Contractor-Government Board established for the purpose of reviewing, evaluating, and disposing of specific non-conforming supplies or services; and, for assuring the initiation and accomplishment of corrective action to preclude recurrence. (Source: MIL-STD 105)

*Measuring and Test Equipment. All devices used to measure, gauge, test, inspect, diagnose, or otherwise examine materials, supplies and equipment to determine compliance with technical requirements. (Source: Proposed DODD on Management of Metrology)

Minor Defect. A defect that is not likely to reduce materially the usability of the unit of product for its intended purpose, or is a departure from established standards having little bearing on the effective use or operation of the unit. (Source: MIL-STD 105)

Minor Defective. A unit of product that contains one or more minor defects but contains no critical or major defect. (Source: MIL-STD 105)

MIS Quality Requirements. The process of organizing a project's objectives, strategies and resources for the (quality) data systems. (Source: PMBOK)

*Nonconformance. The failure of a unit of product to conform to specified requirements for any quality characteristic. (Source: MIL-HDBK H53)

Nonconformity. The nonfulfillment of specified requirements. (Source: ISO 8402)

Normal Inspection. Inspection, under a sampling plan, which is used when there is no evidence that the quality of the product being submitted is better or poorer than the specified quality level. (Source: MIL-HDBK H53)

Objective Quality Evidence. Any statement of fact, either quantitative or qualitative, pertaining to the quality of a product or service based on observations, measurements, or tests which can be verified. (Evidence will be expressed in terms of specific quality requirements or characteristics. These characteristics are identified in drawings, specifications, and other documents which describe the item, process, or procedure.) (Source: MIL-STD 109A)

Off-the-Shelf Items. An item produced and placed in stock by a contractor, or stocked by a distributer, before receiving orders or contracts for its sale. The item may be commercial or produced to military or federal specifications or description. (Source: FAR 46.101)

*One Hundred Percent Inspection. Inspection in which specified characteristics of each unit of product are examined or tested to determine conformance with requirements. (Source: MIL-STD 109A)

Operating Characteristic Curves (OC Curves). The curve of a sampling plan which shows the percentage of lots or batches which may be expected to be accepted under the specified sampling plan for a given process quality. (Source: MIL-STD 105)

*Organization. A company, corporation, firm or enterprise, whether incorporated or not, public or private. (Source: ISO 9004)

Overall Quality Philosophy. The universal belief throughout a company that quality is important and performance is based on conformance to requirements/specifications, based on established quality policies and procedures. These policies and procedures become the basis for collecting facts about a project for study and analysis. (Source: PMBOK)

Ownership of Quality Responsibility. The situation when an individual performing a task has the ultimate responsibility for conformance to the requirements/specifications. (Source: PMBOK)

Pareto Diagram. A graph, particularly popular in non-technical projects, to prioritize the few change areas (often 20 percent of the total) that cause most quality deviations (often 80 percent of the total). (Source: PMBOK)

Percent Defective. The percent defective of any given quantity of units of product is one hundred times the number of defective units of product contained therein divided by the total number of units of product, i.e.: Percent Defective = Number of Defectives x 100 divided by Number of Units Inspected. (Source: MIL-STD 105)

Pre-Award Survey. An evaluation of a prospective contractor's capability to perform under the terms of a proposed contract. (Source: FAR)

Probability of Acceptance. That percentage of inspection lots expected to be accepted when the lots are subjected to a specific sampling plan. (Source: MIL-STD 109A)

Process Average. The average percent of defective or average number of defects per hundred units of product submitted by the supplier for original inspection. (Source: MIL-STD 105)

*Product Liability; Service Liability. A generic term used to describe the onus on a producer or others to make restitution for loss related to personal injury, property damage or other harm caused by a product or service. (Source: ISO 8402)

Product Quality Review. An action by the government to determine that the quality of supplies or services accepted by the government do, in fact, comply with specified requirements. (Source: DODD 4155.11)

Production Permit; Deviation Permit. Written authorization, prior to production or before provision of a service, to depart from specified requirements for a specified quantity or for a specified time. (Source: ISO 8402)

*Qualification. The entire process by which products are obtained from manufacturers or distributors, examined and tested, and then identified as a Qualified Products List. (Source: Defense Standardization Manual 4120.3-M)

*Qualified Product. A product which has been examined and tested and listed on or qualified for inclusion on the applicable Qualified Products List. (Source: Defense Standardization Manual 4120.3-M)

Qualified Product List (QPL). A list of products, qualified under the requirements stated in the applicable specification, including appropriate product identification and test reference with the name and plant address of the manufacturer or distributor, as applicable. (Source: Defense Standardization Manual 4120.3-M)

Quality. The composite of all the attributes or characteristics, including performance, of an item or product. (Source: DODD 4155.11)

*****Quality.** The totality of features and characteristics of a product of service that bear on its ability to satisfy stated or implied needs. (Source: ISO 8402)

Quality. Conformance to requirements. A work product either does or does not meet the requirements. (Source: CII Publication 10-2)

*****Quality Assurance.** All those planned and systematic actions necessary to provide adequate confidence that a product or service will satisfy given requirements for quality. (Source: ISO 8402)

Quality Assurance. A planned and systematic pattern of all actions necessary to provide adequate confidence that the item or product conforms to established technical requirements. (Source: DODD 4155.11)

Quality Assurance (Managerial). The development of a comprehensive program which includes the processes of identifying objectives and strategy, of client interfacing and of organizing and coordinating planned and systematic controls for maintaining established standards. This in turn involves measuring and evaluating performance to these standards, reporting results and taking appropriate action to deal with deviations. (Source: PMBOK)

Quality Assurance Representative (QAR). The individual directly charged with performance of the government procurement quality assurance function at a contractor facility. (Source: MIL-STD 105)

*****Quality Audit.** A systematic and independent examination to determine whether quality activities and related results comply with planned arrangements and whether these arrangements are implemented effectively and are suitable to achieve objectives. (Source: ISO 8402)

*****Quality Control.** The operational techniques and activities that are used to fulfill requirements for quality. (Source: ISO 8402)

Quality Control (QC). A management function whereby control of quality of raw or produced material is exercised for the purpose of preventing production of defective material. (Source: MIL-STD 109A)

Quality Control (Technical). The planned process of identifying established technical specifications for the project and exercising influence through the collection of specific (usually highly technical and standardized) data. The basis for decision on any necessary corrective action is provided by analyzing the data and comparing it to system specifications/requirements. (Source: PMBOK)

Quality Evaluation Methods. The technical process of gathering measured variables or counted data for decision making in the quality process review. (Source: PMBOK)

Quality Loop; Quality Spiral. Conceptual model of interacting activities that influence the quality of a product or service in the various stages ranging from the identification of needs to the assessment of whether these needs have been satisfied. (Source: ISO 8402)

*****Quality Management.** That aspect of the overall management function that determines and implements the quality policy. (Source: ISO 8402)

Quality Management Function. Quality itself is the composite of material attributes (including performance features and characteristics) of the product or service which are required to satisfy the need for which the project is launched. Quality standards may be attained through the sub-functions of quality assurance (Managerial) and quality control (Technical). (Source: PMBOK)

*Quality Plan. A document setting out the specific quality practices, resources and sequence of activities relevant to a particular product, service, contract or project. (Source: ISO 8402)

*Quality Policy. The overall quality intentions and direction of an organization as regards quality, as formally expressed by top management. (Source: ISO-8402)

Quality Process Review. The technical process of using data to decide how the actual project results compare with the quality specifications/requirements. If deviations occur, this analysis may cause changes in the project design, development, use, etc., depending on the decisions of the client, involved shareholders and the project team. (Source: PMBOK)

Quality Program Requirement. The requirement for the establishment and maintenance of a quality program in accordance with MIL-Q-9858. The specification requires that the program shall assure adequate quality throughout all areas of contract performance; for example, design, development, fabrication, processing, assembly, inspection, test, maintenance, packaging, shipping storage, and site installation. (Source: FAR)

*Quality Surveillance. The continuing monitoring and verification of the status of procedures, methods, conditions, processes, products and services, and analysis of records in relation to stated references to ensure that specified requirements for quality are being met. (Source: ISO 8402)

*Quality System. The organizational structure, responsibilities, procedures, processes and resources for implementing quality management. (Source: ISO 8402)

*Quality System Review. A formal evaluation by top management of the status and adequacy of the quality system in relation to quality policy and new objectives resulting from changing circumstances. (Source: ISO 8402)

Random Sample. A sample selected in such a way that each unit of the population has an equal chance of being selected. (Source: MIL-STD 109A)

Reduced Inspection. Inspection under a sampling plan using the same quality level as for normal inspection, but requiring a smaller sample for inspection. (Source: MIL-STD 109A)

Rejection Number. The minimum number of defects or defective units in the sample that will cause rejection of the lot represented by the sample. (Source: MIL-STD 109A)

Reliability. The probability that an item will perform its intended function for a specified interval under stated conditions. (Source: MIL-STD 721)

*Reliability. The ability of an item to perform a required function under stated conditions for a stated period of time. (Source: ISO 8402)

Reliability Assurance. All actions necessary to provide adequate confidence that material conforms to established reliability requirements. (Source: DODD 4155.11)

*Requirements of Society. Requirements including laws, statutes, rules and regulations, codes, environmental considerations, health and safety factors, and conservation of energy and materials. (Source: ISO 9004)

Resubmitted Lot. A lot which has been rejected, subjected to either examination or testing, or both for the purpose of removing all defective units which may or may not be reworked or replaced, and submitted again for acceptance. (Source: MIL-STD 109A)

*Sample. One or more units of product drawn from a lot or batch, the units of the sample being selected at random without regard to their quality. (Source: MIL-STD 105)

Sample, Representative. The number of units selected in proportion to the size of sub-lots or sub-batches, or parts of the lot or batch, identified by some rational criterion. When representative sampling is used, the units from each part of the lot or batch shall be selected at random. (Source: MIL-STD 105)

Sample Size. The number of units of product in the sample selected for inspection. (Source: MIL-STD 105)

Sample Unit. A unit of product selected to be part of a sample. (Source: MIL-STD 109A)

Sampling, Biased. Sampling procedures which will not guarantee a truly representative or random sample. (Source: MIL-STD 109A)

Sampling Frequency (f). The sampling frequency, f, is the ratio between the number of units of product randomly selected for inspection at an inspection station to the number of units of product passing the inspection station. (Source: MIL-HDBK H107)

Sampling Plan. A statement of the sample size or sizes to be used and the associated acceptance and rejection criteria. (Source: MIL-STD 109A)

Sampling Plan, Double. A specific type of attributes sampling plan in which the inspection of the first sample leads to a decision to accept, to reject, or to take a second sample. The inspection of a second sample, when required, then leads to a decision to accept or reject. (Source: MIL-STD 105)

Sampling Plan, Multi-Level, Continuous. A specific type of sampling plan in which the inspection periods of 100 percent inspection and two or more levels of sampling inspection are alternated with the sampling frequency remaining constant or changing on the basis of the inspection result. (Source: MIL-HDBK H106)

Sample Plan, Multiple. A specific type of attributes sampling plan in which a decision to accept or reject an inspection lot may be reached after one or more samples from that inspection lot have been inspected, and will always be reached after not more than a designated number of samples have been inspected. (Source: MIL-STD 105)

Sampling Plan, Sequential. A specific type of sampling plan in which the sample units are selected one at a time. After each unit is inspected, the decision is made to accept, reject, or continue inspection until the acceptance or rejection criteria is met. Sampling terminates when the inspection results of the sample units determine that the acceptance or rejection decision can be made. The sample size is not fixed in advance, but depends on actual inspection results. (Source: MIL-HDBK H53)

Sampling Plan, Single. A specific type of sampling plan in which a decision to accept or reject an inspection lot is based on a single sample. (Source: MIL-STD 105)

Sampling Plan, Single-Level, Continuous. A specific type of sampling plan in which the inspection periods of 100 percent inspection and sampling inspection are alternated with the sampling rate remaining constant. (Source: MIL-HDBK H107)

Screening Inspection. Inspection in which each item of product is inspected for designated characteristics and all defective items are removed. (Source: MIL-STD 109A)

Specification. A document intended primarily for use in procurement, which clearly and accurately describes the essential and technical requirements for items, materials, or services, including the procedures by which it will be determined that the requirements have been met. Specifications for items and materials may also contain preservation, packaging, packing and marking requirements. (Source: Defense Standardization Manual 4120.3-M)

Specification. The document that prescribes the requirements with which the product or services has to conform. (Source: ISO 8402)

*Self-Inspection. The individual performing the task also conducts the measurements to ensure conformance to the requirements/specification. (Source: PMBOK)

Storage Quality Control. The technical inspection of materiel received from vendors which was not previously inspected at source and for which acceptance at destination is required; inspection of materiel returned from consuming installations for return to stores, forwarding to repair facilities, for release to disposal areas; the examination and testing of samples of supplies selected from storage to assess the overall quality of materiel stored, and the identification of previously unidentified materiel in store; and inspection of materiel prior to shipping to using activities. (Source: DODD 4155.13)

Summative Quality Evaluation. The process of determining what lessons have been learned after the project is complete with the objective of documenting behaviors which helped determine, maintain, or increase quality standards and which ones did not. (Source: PMBOK)

Survey, Product Oriented. A review and evaluation to determine the adequacy of the technical requirements relating to quality and product conformance to design intent. (Source: FAR)

Technical Quality Administration. The technical process of establishing the plan for monitoring and controlling the project's satisfactory completion. The plan is designed to include policies and procedures which prevent or correct deviations from requirements/specifications. (Source: PMBOK)

Technical Quality Specifications. The process of establishing the specific project requirements, including execution criteria and technologies, project design, measurement specifications, and material procurement and control, that satisfy the expectations of the client, shareholders, and project team. (Source: PMBOK)

Technical Quality Support. The process of providing technical training and expertise from one or more support groups to a project in a timely manner. (Source: PMBOK)

*Testing. That element of inspection that determines the properties or elements, including functional operation of supplies or their components, by the application of established scientific principles and procedures. (Source: FAR 46.101)

*Total Quality Management (TQM). The consistent integrated orchestration of the total complex of an organization's work processes and activities to achieve continuous improvement in the organization's processes and products. (Source: DOD TQM Master Plan, August, 1988)

*Traceability. The ability to trace the history, application or location of an item or activity, or similar items or activities, by means of recorded identification. (Source: ISO 8402)

Unit of Product. The thing inspected in order to determine its classification as defective or nondefective or to count the number of defects. It may be a single article, a pair, a set, a length, an area, an operation, a volume, a component of an end product, or the end product itself. The unit of product may or may not be the same as the unit of purchase, supply, production, or shipment. (Source: MIL-STD 105)

*Warranty. A promise or affirmation given by a contractor to the government regarding the nature, usefulness, or condition of the supplies or performance of services furnished under the contract. (Source: FAR 46.701)

The bibliography represents all known formal sources of information used in the development of this book. Other sources of an informal nature, to include conversations with individuals, have been used and not specifically identified herein. This formal listing, however, provides a ready reference to many current sources of quality information.

Appendix D

Bibliography

1. Althouse, Lynda M., and George C. Derringer. "It sticks, but will it last? Statistical method provides a more realistic determination of adhesive service life than conventional methods do." *Research & Development*, Vol. 26 (October 1984): 146-149.

2. Anderson, Robert E. "Quality: It's a 'Given' in Today's Marketplace." *Design News*, Vol. 43 (April 20, 1987):44.

3. Barney, Clifford. "Statistical Method Evaluates EE-PROMS." *Electronics Week*, Vol. 57 (July 23, 1984):26-27.

4. Bauer, Betsy. "Warranty warfare: Auto makers lure customers with super long guarantees." *US News & World Report*, Vol. 102 (February 16, 1987):46.

5. Benoit, Ellen. "Who's on First? (Quality control in the semiconductor industry)" *Forbes*, Vol. 134 (December 3, 1984): 224.

6. Berney, Karen. "Industry Seeks Pentagon Changes." *Electronics Week*, Vol. 58 (January 14, 1985):20.

7. Berger, Joan. "In the Service Sector Nothing is 'Free' Anymore." *Business Week* (June 8, 1987):144.

8. Berger, Roger W. *Statistical Process Control: A Guide for Implementation*. New York: Marcel Dekker, Inc., 1986.

9. Berry, Leonard, Valarie A. Zeithaml, and A. Parasuraman. "Quality counts in services, too." *Business Horizons*, Vol. 28 (May-June 1985):44-52.

10. Beverioe, Don. "Quality counts." *Sales and Marketing Management*, Vol. 135 (December 9, 1985):12.

11. Blair, John D., and Carlton J. Whitehead. "Can quality circles survive in the United States?" *Business Horizons*, Vol. 27 (September-October 1984):17-23.

12. Boggs, Robert N. "Survey Shows Productivity and Quality Improve." *Design News*, Vol. 41 (July 8, 1985):115-118.

13. Bowles, Jerry G. "The quality imperative: How winning companies use quality improvement to cut costs, increase productivity, and boost the bottom line." *Fortune*, Vol. 114 (September 29, 1986):61-74.

14. Bowles, Jerry G. "Quality: The competitive advantage. (Special advertising section) *Fortune*, Vol. 116 (September 28, 1987):129-140.

15. Carroll, Ginny, and Mark Miller. "America's Big Risk: Many Facilities Suffer from Bad Management." *Newsweek*, Vol. 109 (April 27, 1987):58-59.

16. Chitty, Marv, and Linda Gelb. "Quality assurance and online searching. *Online*, Vol. 11 (March 1987):110-112.

17. Cleland, David I., and William R. King, *Systems Analysis and Project Management*, 2nd Ed., New York: McGraw-Hill, 1975.

18. Como, Frank W. "Commitment: Key to Improved Quality and Productivity." *Design News*, Vol. 41 (August 1985).

19. Connell, John, and Linda Brice. "Practical quality assurance: Los Alamos National Laboratory has created a quality assurance plan that works." *Datamation*, Vol. 31 (March 1, 1985): 106-110.

20. Connolly, Ray. "New Quality-Control Problems Arise for Hughes in Dispute with Military over Faulty Radar System." *Electronics Week*, Vol. 57 (September 3, 1984):42-43.

21. Corey, Robert L. "Artificial perception gives super vision." *Research & Development*, Vol. 26 (October 1984):142-144.

22. Covault, Craig, "Documentation is involved in delay of shuttle." *Aviation Week and Space Technology*, Vol. 121 (September 24, 1984):14-16.

23. Covault, Craig. "NASA chief admonishes managers on shuttle accident." *Aviation Week and Space Technology*, Vol. 122 (April 1, 1985):25.

24. Crosby, Phillip B. *The Art of Getting Your Own Sweet Way*, 2nd ed. 240 p., 1981.

25. Crosby, Phillip B. *Quality is Free: The Art of Making Quality Free*, 1979.

26. Crosby, Phillip B. *Quality Without Tears: The Art of Hassle Free Management*, 192p., 1984.

27. Doan, Michael. "The view from Main Street: America is slipping (in international trade)." *US News & World Report* , Vol. 102 (February 2, 1987):20-21.

28. Dugan, George. "Thermal analysis supports chemical R&D product quality control: New techniques work for hazards evaluation, stability studies, and characterization." *Research & Development*, Vol. 27 (June 1985):98-103.

29. Ebrahimpour, Maling. "An Examination of Quality Management in Japan: Implications for Management in the United States." *Journal of Operations Management*, Vol. 5, No. 4 (August 1985):419-431.

30. Edson, Daniel V. "Quality on the Upswing." *Design News*, Vol. 40 (September 3, 1984):77-82

31. Engel, Paul G. "Zero defects: Tenent is swept away with program." *Industry Week*, Vol. 227 (December 9, 1985):21.

32. Evans, Michael K. "Boondoggles in the name of competitiveness." *Industry Week*, Vol. 232 (February 9, 1987):72.

33. Feigenbaum, Armand V. "How to compete with quality." *Industry Week*, Vol. 221 (April 2, 1984):8.

34. Feigenbaum, A.V. *Total Quality Control*. 3rd Ed., New York: McGraw-Hill Book Co. 1983.

35. Ferchat, Robert A. "Productivity in a customer vein: Quality, design, organization, education and communication." *Vital Speeches*, Vol. 53 (July 15, 1987):602-605.

36. Fierman, Jaclyn. "Why enrollment is up at Quality College: Executives are flocking to Phillip Crosby's school to learn the principles of operating error-free in factories and offices." *Fortune*, Vol.111 (April 29, 1985):170.

37. Frailery, Fred, and Mary Lord. "Sony's no-baloney boss: Akio Morita talks about trade, competitiveness—and his biggest flub." *US News & World Report* , Vol. 101 (November 17, 1986):57.

38. Garry, Fred W. "The Quality Road to Productivity." *Design News*, Vol. 41 (July 8, 1985):86-89.

39. Garvin, David A. "Competing on the eight dimensions of quality." *Harvard Business Review*, (November-December 1987):101-109.

40. Garvin, David A. "Product quality: An important strategic weapon." *Business Horizons*, Vol. 27 (May-June 1984): 43-46.

41. Goldstein, Mark L. "Statistics come home (finally) in a big way." *Industry Week*, Vol. 222 (July 9, 1984):81.

42. Goldstein, Mark L. "Challenger's lessons: NASA's problems also lurk within industry." *Industry Week*, Vol. 230 (August 18, 1986):20-21.

43. Grant, Eugene L., and Richard S. Leavenworth. *Statistical Quality Control*. New York: McGraw-Hill, 1988.

44. Greenberg, Daniel. "High-tech America's myopic mind-set." *US News & World Report*, Vol. 101 (September 22, 1986):64-65.

45. Grindel, J. Michael. "The Management of Quality in Pharmaceutical R&D Projects." *Proceeding of the Project Management Institute Seminar/Symposium*, October 2-7, 1987: 466-469

46. Grubbs, Judith. "GE workers tell: How we dumped QWL circles." *Labor Today,* Vol. 25 (February 1986):5.

47. Guterl, Fred V. "Quality goes high tech: As automation takes over industry is achieving dramatic improvements in product quality." *Business Month,* Vol. 129 (May 1987):44-45.

48. Hall, Robert W. *Zero Inventories.* Dow Jones-Irmin, Homewood, Illinois, 1983: pp. 329.

49. Harrington, H. James. *The Improvement Process: How America's Leading Companies Improve Quality.* McGraw-Hill book Company, New York, 1987, pp. 239.

50. Hamburg, Morris. *Statistical Analysis for Decision Making*, Second Edition, by Harcourt Brace Jovanovich, Inc., 1977.

51. Hart, Christopher W.L., and Gregory D. Casserly. "Quality: A Brand-New, Time-Tested Strategy." *The Cornell Hotel and Restaurant Administration Quarterly* (November 1985):52-63.

52. Hartman, Raymond S. "Product quality and market efficiency: The effect of product recalls on resale prices and firm valuation." *Review of Economics and Statistics,* Vol. 69 (May 1987):367-372.

53. Hayes, Robert H., and Steven C. Wheelwright, *Link Manufacturing Process and Product Life Cycles,* Harvard Business Review, January-February 1979, pp. 133-40.

54. Heizer, Jay, and Barry Render. *Production and Operations Management,* Allyn & Bacon, Inc., 1988

55. Hill, George. "An expectation of excellence." *Business Horizons,* Vol. 28 (September-October 1985):26-27.

56. Helliwell, John. "Inland Steel is Revitalizing via Automation: Goals are Quality Control, Cutting Inventory Stockpiles." *PC Week,* Vol. 4 (April 7, 1987):C1-2.

57. Hines, Richard D. "Statistical Quality Control Meets Industry Demands." *Design News,* Vol. 40 (November 18, 1984):13.

58. Imai, M. *Kaizen: The Key to Japan's Competitive Success.* Random House, New York, 1986.

59. Ingle, Sud. *In Search of Perfection: How to Create/Maintain/Improve Quality* by Prentice-Hall, Inc., 1985.

60. Imberman, Woodruff. "The golden nuggets on the factory floor (employee suggestions, productivity, etc.)" *Business Horizons,* Vol. 29 (July-August 1986):63-69.

61. Jacobson, Allen F. "Quality at Work." *Design News,* Vol. 41 (July 8, 1985):30- 34.

62. Jamieson, Archbalt. *Introduction to Quality Control,* Prentice-Hall Company, 1982.

63. Jones, Peter. "The American who saved Japan. (W. Edwards Deming)" *Scholastic Update,* Vol. 119 (April 6, 1987):8.

64. Juran, J. M. *Planning for Quality.* 341 p. 1987, The Free Press, New York

65. Juran, Joseph M. *Quality Control Handbook,* Rev 3rd Ed. 1600 p. 1974, McGraw-Hill

66. Juran, Joseph M., and Frank M. Gryna, Jr. *Quality Planning & Analysis: From Product Development Through Use.* 2nd Ed. (Illus), McGraw-Hill, 1980.

67. Kindel, Stephen. "The Workshop Economy." *Forbes,* Vol. 133 (April 30, 1984):62-66.

68. Kahwati, Ghassan, and Paul Law. "Machine vision system assures product quality: Electronic imaging setup finds flaws, adjusts production equipment." *Research & Development,* Vol. 28 (February 1986):4-5.

69. Kasza, K.E., J.J. Oras and John Bagby. "What's moving, and does it affect your product?" *Research & Development,* Vol. 30 (March 1988):62-66.

70. Kindel, Stephen. "Does Your Car Have a Fan Belt? Quality Has always been viewed as a problem of managing." *Forbes,* Vol. 134 (December 3, 1984):222-224.

71. Kirkman, Jane L. "Hey, Ms. Smith, The computer's doing something funny again!" *Clearing House,* Vol. 60 (September 1986):30-36.

72. Klass, Phillip J. "Navy planning additional teardown inspections like those with Phoenix." *Aviation Week and Space Technology,* Vol. 122 (June 3, 1985):394- 399.

73. Kloppenborg, Tim, and Francis M. Webster, Jr., "Responsibility for Quality in a Project," *PM NETwork,* February 1990, pp. 25-27.

74. Kozicharow, Eugene. "USAF emphasizing technology to improve quality assurance. (part 1)." *Aviation Week and Space Technology,* Vol. 121 (December 3, 1984):78-80.

75. Krider, James W., Jr. "Double-check your quality assurance: Tester for IC burn-in boards catches faults in circuitry used to detect component flaws." *Research & Development,* Vol. 27 (October 1985):114- 115.

76. Kroger, Joseph J. "Expanding the Quality Circles." *Design News,* Vol. 41 (July 8, 1985):80-83.

77. Kuzela, Lad. "Executives join top-down pursuit of productivity." *Industry Week,* Vol. 221 (May 28, 1984):39-41.

78. Kuzela, Lad. "Whitecollar automation: Statistical technique to boost performance." *Industry Week,* Vol. 223 (November 12, 1984):21.

79. Kuzela, Lad. "Employee participation: Labor-management togetherness increases." *Industry Week,* Vol. 228 (December 9, 1985):30.

80. Kyd, Charles W. "Quality nightmares: You can't ignore a quality problem until 'things get better' - because they won't." *Inc.,* Vol. 9 (October 1987):155-157.

81. Lawler, Edward E., Jr. "Quality Circles after the fad." *Harvard Business Review.* Vol. 63 (January-February 1985):64-71.

82. Lyman, Jerry. "Moving wafer inspection into the fast lane." *Electronics,* Vol. 60 (March 5, 1987):63-64.

83. Main, Jeremy. "The trouble with managing Japanese-style." *Fortune,* Vol. 109 (April 2, 1984):50-54.

84. Main, Jeremy. "The curmudgeon who talks tough on quality." *Fortune,* Vol. 109 (June 25, 1984):118-122.

85. Main, Jeremy. "Under the spell of the quality gurus: These consultants get up to $10,000 a day to help companies improve their products." *Fortune,* Vol. 114 (August 18, 1986):30-33.

86. Malcolm, Donald G. "Reliability Maturity Index (RMI) - An Extension of PERT into Reliability Management. *The Journal of Industrial Engineering,* January-February 1963, pp. 3-12.

87. Mansir, Brian E., and Nicholas R. Schacht. *An Introduction to Continuous Improvement Process: Principles & Practices.* Unpublished, c.1989.

88. Mayer, Daniel J. "Beyond the numbers: What price automation?" *Industry Week,* Vol. 228 (January 6, 1986):12.

89. Mercer, James L. "Improving employee productivity." *American City and County,* Vol. 100 (October 1985):68-72.

90. Michaels, Jack D. "The importance and impact of standards: Elements in global competition." *Vital Speeches,* Vol. 53 (May 1, 1987):441-444.

91. Michaels, Mark. "Quality teamwork stays on target." *American City County,* Vol. 100 (April 1985):66-68.

92. Moad, Jeff. "Quality and productivity improvements: U.S. and foreign company experiences." *Library Journal,* Vol. 32 (June 1, 1986):44-46.

93. Nayak, R. Ranganath, and John M. Ketteringham. *Breakthrough!* Rawson Associates: New York, 1986, pp. 371.

94. Norden, Peter V. "On the Anatomy of Development Projects." *IRE Transactions on Engineering Management,* March 1960, pp. 34-42.

95. O'Donnell, Robert J. "Quality circles—The latest fad or a real winner?" *Business Horizons,* Vol. 27 (May-June 1984):48-52.

96. Odiorne, George S. "The trouble with Japanese management systems." *Business Horizons,* Vol. 27 (July-August 1984):17-23.

97. Pallatio, John. "At Pratt & Whitney interactive video exercises quality control: PC-based workstations provide a cost-effective training solution enabling assembly-line workers to spot defective products." *PC Week,* Vol. 4 (June 16, 1987):43-44.

98. Pall, Gabriel A. *Quality Process Management*, Prentice-Hall (1987):304.

99. Pascarella, Perry. "Quality circles uncoil: Changing concept impacts corporate culture." *Industry Week*, Vol. 221 (April 30, 1984):16.

100. Pascarella, Perry. "Smaller firms pace growth of quality circles." *Industry Week*, Vol. 229 (April 14, 1986):20.

101. Pascarella, Perry. "Is the boss committed to quality?" *Industry Week*, Vol. 234 (August 24, 1987):9.

102. Paul, William. "Retooling the shop floor for quality." *Industry Week*, Vol. 226 (August 5, 1985):14.

103. Pennar, Karen. "America's Quest Can't be Half-Hearted." *Business Week* (June 8, 1987):136.

104. Perrow, Charles, *Organizational Analysis: A Sociological View*, London: Tavistock Publications, 1970.

105. Peters, Tom, *Thriving on Chaos*. New York: Harper & Row, Publishers, Inc., 1987.

106. Peters, Thomas J. "More expensive, but worth it." *US News & World Report* , Vol. 100 (February 3, 1986): 54.

107. Peters, Thomas J., and Perry Pascarella. "Searching for excellence: The winners deliver on value." *Industry Week*, Vol. 221 (April 16, 1984):61-62.

108. Port, Otis, and Mimi Bluestone. "The Push for Quality: To Beat Imports the U.S. Must Improve its Products. This means a whole new approach to manufacturing." *Business Week*, (June 8, 1987):130-135.

109. Port, Otis. "How to Make it Right the First Time." *Business Week*, (June 8, 1987):142-143.

110. Podolsky, Joseph L. "The quest for quality: Current quality assurance tools may be inadequate, but it's crucial that we use them and improve upon them." *Datamation*, Vol. 31 (March 1, 1985):119-123.

111. Rohan, Thomas M. "Quest for quality: Computers, lasers revolutionizing inspection." *Industry Week*, Vol. 221 (April 30, 1984):29.

112. Rohan, Thomas M. "Customers say quality program helps make sales." *Industry Week*, Vol. 222 (September 3, 1984):29-30.

113. Rohan, Thomas M. "Quality picks up: Everybody wants to get into the act." *Industry Week*, Vol. 227 (October 28, 1985):20-21.

114. Rohan, Thomas M. "Laboratories, Inc. Quality control case study)," *Industry Week*, Vol. 229 (June 23, 1986):54-58.

115. Rohan, Thomas M. "Quality helps sell, too (as well as cuts costs)." *Industry Week*, Vol. 233 (April 6, 1987):47-50.

116. Rohan, Thomas M. "Japan hasn't lost lead; U.S. efforts still miss the mark." *Industry Week*, Vol. 234 (September 7, 1987):28.

117. Rohan, Thomas M. "Mandate rather than motivate: The team must be assigned to do a job, not motivated or inspired." *Industry Week*, Vol. 236 (May 2, 1988):58-59.

118. Sammons, Donna. "Driving a hard bargain. (automobile industry adopts statistical process control)" *Carpenter*, Vol. 7 (May 1985):165-167.

119. Scanlon, Terrence. "We want to work with companies, not against them." *US News & World Report* , Vol. 98 (April 15, 1985):74.

120. Shetty, Y. Krishna, and Vernon M. Buehler. "Quality and productivity improvements: U.S. and foreign company experiences." *Business Economics*, Vol. 19 (July 1984):63-64.

121. Shiller, Zachary, and William J. Hampton. "Why Image Counts: A Tale of Two Industries." *Business Week* (June 8, 1987):138-140.

122. Shutsker, Gary. "Thought I Was a Madman." *Forbes*, Vol. 137 (May 19, 1986):100-101.

123. Smeltzer, Larry R., and Ben L. Kedia. "Knowing the ropes: Organizational requirements for quality circles." *Business Horizons*, Vol. 28 (July-August 1985):30-34.

124. Smith, Bill. "The Motorola Story." A paper distributed by Motorola that describes the 1988 Malcolm Baldrige National Quality Award, c. 1989.

125. Stair, Ralph M., Jr., and Barry Render. *Production and Operations Management: A Self-Correcting Approach*, Second Edition, Allyn and Bacon, 1980.

126. Staples, E.R. "The quest for quality information." *Office Administration and Automation*, Vol. 45 (November 1984):82.

127. Stefenides, E.J. "Electro-optical System Simplifies Inspection." *Design News*, Vol. 41 (May 20, 1985):116-119.

128. Steiner, George A., and William G. Ryan, *Industrial Project Management*, New York: Macmillan, 1968.

129. Taguchi, Genichi. "How Japan Defines Quality." *Design News*, Vol. 41 (July 8, 1985):99-103.

130. Tenopir, Carol. "Quality control." *Library Journal*, Vol. 112 (February 15, 1987):124-125.

131. Thamhain, Hans J. "Validating Technical Project Plans," *Project Management Journal*, December 1989, 43-50.

132. Thompson, Carl. "Quality sells itself." *Sales and Marketing Management"*, Vol. 138 (June 1987):13.

133. Thompson, Donald B. "Back to basics: Confronting the competitiveness challenge." *Industry Week*, Vol. 223 (December 10, 1984):73-77.

134. Trepanier, Peter. "Quality begins with participative involvement."*Industry Week*, Vol. 223 (October 1, 1984):14.

135. Tyler, Michael A. "Hard facts on hardware reliability? A new system that supplies reliability data also gives extra clout in dealing with hardware vendors." *Datamation*, Vol. 30 (October 1, 1984):82-89.

136. Waller, Larry. "Stringent Specification and Burdensome Documentation Create a Quality Problem for Parts That Meet Military Standards." *ElectronicsWeek*, Vol. 57 (July 23, 1984):22-23.

137. Walton, Richard E. "From Control to Commitment in the Workplace." *Harvard Business Review* (March-April 1985):76-84.

138. Webster, Francis M., Jr. *The Management of Projects - An Examination of the State-of-the-Art as Represented by Current Literature*, Ph.D. Dissertation, Michigan State University, 1978.

139. Webster, Francis M., Jr. "Micro Characteristics of an Activity and its Performance," *Proceedings of the Project Management Institute*, Drexel Hill, PA, October 1979.

140. Weidenbaum, Murray. "Learning to compete." *Business Horizons*, Vol. 29 (September-October 1986):2-12.

141. Wheaton, James W. "The Quality Quest." *Design News*, Vol. 43 (April 20, 1987):46-51.

142. Woodward, J., *Industrial Organization: Theory and Practice*, London: Oxford University Press, 1965.

143. Zeiders, Beth Bandy, and Marie Sivak. "Quality Circles From A to Z: King Arthur to Theory A." *Clearing House*, Vol. 59 (November 1985):123-124.

144. Zuesse, Eric. "Quality: How to know it and get it." *Library Journal*, Vol. 111 (March 1, 1986):92.

AUTHORS NOT IDENTIFIED

145. Contract monitor. *Aviation Week and Space Technology*, Vol. 121 (September 3, 1984):267.

146. *Costs of Quality Deviations in Design and Construction*, Publication 10-1, Construction Industry Institute, Austin, TX, January 1989:26.

147. Do U.S. firms use a double standard? *US News & World Report* , Vol. 97 (December 17, 1984):26.

148. Five cases that changed American society. *Scholastic Update*, Vol. 117 (November 30, 1984):19-20.

149. Hughes resumes deliveries of two radars. *Aviation Week and Space Technology*, Vol. 121 (October 15, 1984):26.

150. Let the 'Big Q' be your umbrella. (Quality is everyone's responsibility and involves all transactions) *Nation's Business*, Vol. 74 (July 1986):70-71.

151. The Long Road Back to Quality. *Business Week*, (June 8, 1987):158.

152. Malcolm Baldrige Award promotes quality as a top national priority. *Business America*, Vol. 109 (March 28, 1988):36.

153. *Measuring the Cost of Quality in Design and Construction.* Publication 10-2, Construction Industry Institute, Austin, TX, May 1989:18.

154. Microchip test problem halts weapon deliveries. *Aviation Week and Space Technology*, Vol. 121 (September 17, 1984):23-24.

155. *The Project Management Body of Knowledge*, Drexel Hill, PA: Project Management Institute, 1987.

156. *Quality Assurance*, Office Electronics, Inc. Business Forms.

157. *Quality in the Constructed Project: A Guideline for Owners, Designers, and Constructors.* Volume 1. American Society of Civil Engineers, New York, 1988:192.

158. The renaissance of American quality. (Advertising Supplement) *Fortune*, Vol. 112 (October 14, 1985):166-174.

159. Signetics Corp. stops shipments of suspect military circuit products. *Aviation Week and Space Technology*, Vol. 121 (November 12, 1984):25.

160. *Statistical Process Control.* Rieker Management Systems, Los Gatos, CA, 1985.

161. USAF approves Hughes plan to correct quality problems. *Aviation Week and Space Technology*, Vol. 121 (November 12, 1984):24.

162. USAF stops Hughes payments for missiles built at Tucson. *Aviation Week and Space Technology*, Vol. 121 (August 27, 1984):24.

U.S. Department of Commerce

National Institute of Standards and Technology
Gaithersburg, MD 20899

163. *Applications Guidelines 1989: Malcolm Baldrige National Quality Award.* 1988: 31.

164. *Applications Guidelines 1990: Malcolm Baldrige National Quality Award.* 1989: 36.

165. *Applications Guidelines 1991: Malcolm Baldrige National Quality Award.* 1990: 42.

U.S. Department of Defense

For Defense Standards/Specifications (Mil Stds, Mil Specs):
  Commanding Officer
  Naval Publications and Forms Center
  Philadelphia Naval Base
  Philadelphia, PA 19120-5099
  Customer Service Tel.: (215) 697-2179   Order Information Tel.: (215) 697-1189/1195
  Fax Number: (215) 697-2978
For DoD Directives and Instructions:
  National Technical Information Service
  5285 Port Royal Road
  Springfield, VA 22161
  Document Sales Desk Tel.: (703) 487-4650
or
  The U.S. Army Library
  The Pentagon
  Washington, D.C.
or
  Defense Systems Management College
  Attn: Library
  Fort Belvoir, VA 22060

166. Military Handbook. *Guide for Attribute Lot Sampling Inspection and MIL-STD-105.* MIL-HDBK-53-1A, 1 February 1982.

167. Military Handbook. *Sampling Procedures and Tables for Life and Reliability Testing (Based On Exponential Distribution).* Quality Control and Reliability Handbook (Interim) H108, 29 April 1960.

168. Military Handbook. *Statistical Procedures for Determining Validity of Suppliers' Attributes Inspection.* Quality Control and Reliability Handbook (Interim) H-109, 6 May 1960.

169. Military Specification. *Quality Program Requirements.* MIL-Q-9858A, 16 December 1963, with Amendment 2 of 8 March 1985.

170. Military Specification. *Inspection System Requirements.* MIL-I-45208A, 16 December 1963.

171. Military Standard 690B, *Failure Rate Sampling Plans and Procedures.* 17 April 1968.

172. Military Standard 781D, *Reliability Testing for Engineering Development, Qualification, and Production.* 17 October 1986.

173. Military Standard 785B, *Reliability Program for Systems and Equipment Development and Production.* 15 September 1980.

174. Military Standard 790D, *Reliability Assurance Program for Electronic Parts Specifications.* 30 May 1986.

175. Military Standard 1235B, *Single- and Multi-Level Continuous Sampling Procedures and Table for Inspection by Attributes.* 10 December 1981.

176. Military Standard 1535A(USAF), *Supplier Quality Assurance Program Requirements.* 1 February 1974.

177. Military Standard 2074(AS), *Failure Classification for Reliability Testing.* 15 February 1978.

178. *Systems Engineering Management Guide.* Defense Systems Management College, December 1986.

International Organization for Standardization (ISO)
1, ru de Zurich
Case Postale 56
CH-1121 Geneva 20, Switzerland
Secretary General: Lawrence D Eicher,   Ph. 22 316429

179. ISO Standard 8402, *Terms and Definitions.*

180. ISO Standard 9000, *Quality Management and Quality Assurance Standards: Guidelines for Selection and Use.*

181. ISO Standard 9001, *Quality Systems: Model for Quality Assurance in Design/Development, Production, Installation and Servicing.*

182. ISO Standard 9002, *Quality Systems: Model for Quality Assurance in Production and Installation.*

183. ISO Standard 9003, *Quality Systems: Model for Quality Assurance in Final Inspection and Test.*

184. ISO Standard 9004, *Quality Management and Quality System Elements: Guidelines.*

Lewis R. Ireland, *president of L.R. Ireland Associates, specializes in quality and project management consulting. He has more than eighteen years of experience in planning and implementing projects ranging in value from $6,500 to $178,000,000 for both the public and private sectors. His education includes a doctorate in business administration from Columbia Pacific University, a masters degree in systems management from Florida Institute of Technology, and a bachelors degree from Benedictine College. Dr. Ireland is a Fellow of the Project Management Institute and a recipient of the Project Management Institute's Person of the Year and Distinguished Contribution awards.*